'Everything from daft to downright dangerous. Buy it, read it and enjoy it!'
ANNA MURBY, BBC RADIO

'Perfect fodder for an amusing and thought-provoking collection of anecdotal stories.'
WRITERS NEWS

'There is a touch of Phineas Fogg about this work which inspires rapid page-turning.'
DOVER WEB

'A compelling read.'
TRISHA JACKSON, PAN MACMILLAN

'Anyone who has read Bill Bryson will find this an astringent alternative.'
BRIAN BOLLEN, WRITER/EDITOR

'It will surely leave some readers, with their own wanderlust aroused, wondering: Could I? Should I? And if not now, when?'
JOAN RILEY, AbsoluteWrite.com (USA)

ONE WAY or ANOTHER

*A travelogue
of true adventure
(and misadventure)
stories*

RICHARD MEREDITH
The 'Balding Backpacker'

MercuryBooks

Published by Mercury Books, Newport Pagnell, Bucks, MK16 0DD, England.

The right of Richard Meredith to be identified as the author of this work has been asserted by him in accordance with the Copyright, Designs and Patents Act, 1988.

First published February 2002 by Mercury Books and AuthorsOnLine.
Second edition published June 2002 by Mercury Books.

All information is believed current and correct at time of writing. Some names have been omitted by request or changed to avoid embarrassment.

This work is the copyright of the author and may not be reproduced, stored in a retrieval system or transmitted in any form by any means, electronic, mechanical, photocopying, recording or otherwise, without the written permission of the copyright owners: Mercury Books and Richard Meredith.

Copyright © Richard Meredith and Mercury Books.

All photographs are the work of the author and his copyright except the political candidates in *Has Anyone Seen the President?* which were provided by the relevant party offices, John Lennon and the first train into Vancouver in *Still on Track*, provided by Canadian Pacific, and pictures for *Name-dropping with the Greatest* by VIP Tours of 9830 Bellanca Avenue, Los Angeles CA 90045. The help of each of them is gratefully acknowledged.

In the event of any question arising as to the ownership of any other materials or illustrations, please contact: Mercury Books at Newport Pagnell MK16 0DD, England.

Picture scanning: Harvest Studios, Northampton NN1 4AQ.
Editorial co ordination: Sheila Plater (T: 01908.566426).
Visual consultant: Karen Parker, AGFA UK Digital Photographer of the Year 2000/01.
Designed and Typeset in New Baskerville, Poppl Laudatio and Officina Sans by:
Evergreen Graphics, Aldwick, West Sussex PO21 4DU.

ISBN 0-9541432-0-5   Library of Congress Control Number: 2002103031

British Library Dewey Classification: 910.4' 092.

Manufactured separately in Great Britain and in the USA by Lightning Source.

Richard Meredith is a journalist and writer whose background has mainly been in newspapers and the business press. He was born and educated in England and first tried accountancy, but soon found it wasn't for him. After a year hitch-hiking round Europe he began a career in journalism which eventually led him to the *Daily Express*. He left to start a weekly newspaper with friends and later began his own company producing business magazines, industry reviews and yearbooks. He lives sometimes in Spain but mostly in Buckinghamshire, England.

Front Cover Pictures: Quebec City, Canada: This "any whichway" signpost is outside the *Hotel de la place d'Armes* on the *rue Sainte-Anne* (aka Anne d'Autriche, Queen of France 1601–1666) opposite the *Cathedrale de la Sante-Trinite*. The cathedral dates back to 1804 and is the oldest anglican cathedral outside the British Isles. It is a replica of St.Martin's-in-the-Field in London.

British Airways ticket: Last leg (Boston, USA – Heathrow, UK) of the OneWorld travel package.

Distribution/Publisher-sites/Ordering:

Ask your local bookstore or online stockist quoting author's name and/or book title and/or ISBN reference:
0-9541432-0-5
Principle distributors and publisher-sites are:

For printed copy orders, visit:

UK, Europe, Asia :
Mercury Books, Newport Pagnell MK16 0DD, England
T/F: +44 (0)1908. 618439
E: mercurybooks@btconnect.com
http://www.mercurybooks.co.uk

North & South America :
Booklocker.com, PO Box 2399, Bangor, Maine ME 04402, USA
F: +1 207. 262. 5544
E: orders@booklocker.com
http://www.booklocker.com

For electronic book purchases, visit:

Canada :
http://www.travelunbound.com

USA :
http://www.booklocker.com

Australia :
http://www.ebookland.net

UK :
http://www.authorsonline.co.uk

PREFACE

This travelogue covers a year which ended on May 15 2001. I have attempted to update stories written before then with any subsequent events or developments of importance. These are shown as Footnotes. Anything after May 15 came too late for inclusion.

However, by taking advantage of a second printing of the book, I have been able to make an exception to this by revising the story about my visit to the Twin Tower buildings in Manhattan (–see NEW YORK'S DOUBLE VISION on Page 100).

Richard Meredith

TIME WAITS FOR NO MAN...

Perth, Western Australia:

Below this ancient clock in Perth's main shopping mall is an inscription which reads –

> *"No minute gone
> comes ever back again.
> Take heed and see ye
> nothing do in vain."*

Ottawa, Canada:

On the sidewalk in Rideau Street going east between buildings 256 – 258 is this inscription on a paving stone –

> *"This land was in my trust.
> I had one year to build a tiny home
> to prove my sincerity and care
> for the place. I built nothing
> and lost it forever."*
>
> J.DOE, 1826

ONE WAY or ANOTHER
A travelogue of true adventure
(and misadventure) stories

*For Clare and Robert
– whose journeys have only just begun;
and Wendy M*

These stories have been written for some special people around the world who have helped me on my travels with their encouragement, love and kindness. I am especially grateful to several journalists and publishing people who have helped me with the project: Geoff and Tony in the UK; Veenu in India; Laura, Doug and Larry in the USA; Erik in Canada; and Geoff M in Australia. Also to Mike in San Francisco for his amazing IT skills.

Special thanks also to:
Ed, Connie, Heather and Seminolemom1; Julia; uncle Mike, and Bullmoose Liz in the USA. Pauly, Isabelle and Martin; Chris and Katrina; Mon, Howie and Chris in Canada; "mother hen" in Spain; Daboo in India; Kristine in Barbados; Rob in Indonesia; Nada in Egypt; Ann and Anan in Thailand; Dani in Switzerland; Bubbles + L & O, brother Nick, coz Tony, Brian, Wendy A, Steve and Dave in the UK; Renadi in Fiji; Justin in Dubai; and Manuel and Silvia in Argentina.

*"Without you lot,
I might have caught the next plane home."*
RICHARD MEREDITH

CONTENTS

INTRODUCTION	1

North America

AND THE WALL CAME TUMBLING DOWN Quebec City, Canada	11
STILL ON TRACK Canada	23
HAS ANYONE SEEN THE PRESIDENT? United States	29

    1. It's a hell of a job
    2. Oops, I'll read that again
    3. Worms under the rock
    4. Close, but no cigar
    5. Wearing the hair-shirt

SMALL REVOLUTION STRIKES THE KEYS Marathon, Florida	51
BUMS, ALIENS AND THE URBAN POOR California	59
SHAKEN BY AN ECONOMIC EARTHQUAKE San Francisco	67
NAME-DROPPING WITH THE GREATEST Los Angeles	75

PASSING THOUGHTS... PASSING THOUGHTS...
*A miscellany of the bizarre, the unusual and
even the interesting, from around the world*   begins 83

South America, Asia & the Pacific

BAG-NAPPED IN ARGENTINA Buenos Aires, Argentina	103

ONE WAY or ANOTHER

GUNFIGHT IN PARADISE	109
Vitu Levu, Fiji	
1. Journalists are born not made	
2. Exclusive!Mutiny at the barracks	
3. Running the gauntlet with Bull-neck	
JUST CALL ME FRANK	127
Queenstown, New Zealand	
GOING FOR GOLD Oi! Oi! Oi!	135
Sydney, New South Wales	
TAKING THE PLUNGE	141
Cairns, Queensland	
THROWING FRIZBEES AT THE MOON	147
Broome, Western Australia	
THINGS THAT GO BUMP IN THE NIGHT	157
Chumporn, Thailand	
JEWEL IN A TARNISHED CROWN	161
Bali, Indonesia	
EAST GOES WEST FOR NEW-AGE WOMEN	167
Delhi, India	
AND THE SURVEY SAYS...	173
Mumbai, India	
LIFE IN THE FAST LANE	179
Cairo, Egypt	
APPENDIX	
These we have loved...	
Recommended places to stay or visit	
1. Streets	183
2. Hotels	184
3. Boats and watery bits	186
APPENDIX – 1 Newspaper story	187
Vitu Levu, Fiji	
APPENDIX – 2 Newspaper story	191
Sydney Olympics	
APPENDIX – 3 Newspaper story	193
Train ride in India	

ONE WAY or ANOTHER

A travelogue of true adventure (and misadventure) stories

RICHARD MEREDITH

Introduction

"I THINK your bum's the best bit." The voice came from the top bunk. It was Liz. She was surveying me, squinty-eyed from under a heap of crumpled blankets.

There were eight of us in the dormitory at the backpacker's hostel in downtown Sydney. The odour in the room was a fusion of stale beer, strange cigarettes and gorgonzola footwear. On the floor were anthills of discarded clothes draped over rucksacks.

I was trying to hoick my jeans up under my "Sydney's not for softies" T-shirt. Liz had obviously been watching me dress. Being an Aussie, subtlety gets an outing about as often as cucumber sandwiches without crusts.

To be honest, she shouldn't have been in here. Strictly single-sex dorms, said the rules (and no, that didn't mean you could only do it once – I had already tried the joke on the sour-faced receptionist). Positively no visitors after 10pm either.

But the thing is, if you're in Sydney for the Olympics and the whole place is one big party that's been rocking round-the-clock for a fortnight... well, who's to worry if some rules get bent bigger than the curve in a boomerang?

In fact, I was the odd one out. A pom; and not just an ordinary pom either. A novelty pom. Balding, the wrong side of middle-age (at a stretch, but not yet, thank God, at a stroke), a little paunchy. "So how come you're in with us backpackers then mate?" says Liz.

She was more like the norm in the dorm. Single, not much more than 21, carefree. She'd chucked in her job and caught the next plane down here when the action started; just wanted to be part of the fun. And what a snip that hostel was: only Aus $30 a night for a bed in George Street when word was that every room in the city had been sold out for months? We had all been lucky to find it. No worries cobber.

Dorms are part of the scene when you become a road warrior. So are hotels and motels and B&Bs, and sleeping bags on floors, bench seats in airports and reclining crick-in-the-necks on trains and planes. Like the hostel rules in Sydney, you have to be prepared to bend a bit.

Everyone loves a holiday. A couple of weeks here, a couple there. More if you're lucky. But to take a whole year off and go globe-trotting – now that's different. "Oh, you are so lucky. That's something I've always wanted to do." If I've been told it once, I've been told it a hundred times. And yes, I have been lucky. Make no mistake, being a world traveller is a lifetime's experience.

The truth, of course, is that only a very few get the chance to take 12 months out of their lives and – like Liz and me – just upsticks and go walkabout. For some, the chance comes in the "gap year" while waiting for university. Or maybe the year after finishing there – a kind of cathartic final fling before responsibility closes in. Or maybe at the other end of life when travel can be planned into those long-awaited days of retirement. But, by then, maybe being a deck-chair lizard would describe the experience better.

When my chance came, I was no longer a youngster, nor yet – as they call them in America – a senior. I was at one of those crossroads in life which happen to us all. The business into which I had put my heart and soul for 20 years, had been sold. Not for a lot, but enough to allow me to rough it with a smooth edge for a year. My private life had become a mess. I needed a new direction.

So why not just do it? Grab the get-up-and-go. Bite the bullet. Grasp the nettle. Pack those bags and leave it all behind?

Richard (what a fine name) at the travel shop laughed at my plan. "Well, you're certainly not my usual type of client." His tone was loaded with an honours degree in understatement. "Write a book you reckon? Mmm... by the time you come back I'll bet you'll have enough material to fill a library."

I was up at dawn to drive all the way to Cheshire; better get used to seeing the sun come up, I had told myself – and besides, there was no way I could sort out this little adventure on the telephone.

Richard's company is one of only a few in the UK to specialise in round-the-world trips like mine. Now I know why. I took up his time, and his office, for the whole day.

INTRODUCTION

Which way next, partner?

The value is remarkable. Two or three groups of major airlines offer worldwide travel packages. Originally I think it was a philanthropic gesture to help young people broaden their horizons. But these days, as they say, everyone is only as old as they feel. And I felt pretty frisky.

My consortium was the Oneworld Group – an alliance which includes big-name carriers like British Airways, Cathay Pacific, American Airlines and Qantas. There were a few basic rules in the deal, Richard explained: I could only fly where my group's planes went; could only go round in one direction, was restricted to a maximum flying mileage; could only visit six (of the seven) continents; and my returning plane to Heathrow had to be in the air until at least one minute after midnight on the anniversary of my departure. In each case, Richard warned, yes, I could break the rules – like fly with other airlines, go the wrong way, or add extra journeys. But those extras would be at "proper" rates and they would cost me dear. *Fair enough then.* He would book provisional flight dates for me that day, Richard said, because it would set out a structure to my trip. I should try to keep to them but, with enough notice, I could make alterations and they would probably still be OK. *Right you are then.*

ONE WAY or ANOTHER

As I said, it took a whole day to sort it out. But by the end of it, I had a route which took me first to Egypt, then Dubai in the Gulf, then India, Nepal, Hong Kong, Thailand, Singapore, Australia, New Zealand, the USA (west coast), the Caribbean, USA (east coast), Canada and home to the UK. The ticket cost just £ 1,199*.

Richard is the Charles Atlas of adventure planning; a kind of been-there-done-that, world-weary veteran with a mind like a gazetteer and a memory better than any compendium of airline timetables. Occasionally, when some obscure fact or detail eluded him, the computer soon flashed up the answer. But it wasn't often.

And it wasn't just his knowledge that mattered. He weighed me up, too. As a person, I mean. He suggested all the things he knew would interest me; and talked me out of those that wouldn't. There's some mighty fishy places in the world when it's your oyster. By close of play I had got a list – not just of the places I was going, but what I should do when I got there. "You'll enjoy yourself," said Richard as we waited for the itinerary sheet to print out. "That's one of the best I've ever put together."

I signed the final papers to sell the business on March 17. There would be bits and pieces to tie up after that, but, hopefully, not too many. Now, with my journey-plan fixed, I could send off for visas, an international driving licence, check out my insurance, get myself more jabs than was healthy for me ("India, he's going to India," the nurses muttered at my local clinic), let out the house, sort out my papers, make some investments, see the bank manager, update my will (well, you never know do you?), sign over a power of attorney to my brother, buy some new clothes, mosquito deterrents ("India, India," they muttered), a first-aid kit, a set of stout bags... and about a zillion other things.

I had set D-day with Richard for May 15 – just two months to get everything done. "Wow, you're pushing it a bit aren't you," he said. And I knew I was. "But if I leave it any longer something's bound to happen," I professed, "you know how it is with us middle-aged teenagers."

I was also sure, although I didn't say so, that if I gave myself too

---

* This was not, unfortunately, the full extent of my travel costs! Extras included trips to Malaysia and Indonesia (Bali), a Christmas/New Year detour to Spain, France, Switzerland and the UK, plus internal flights in Australia, Canada and the USA. There were also car hire charges and bus and train fares.

INTRODUCTION

long to think about it, I would find a reason to chicken out – despite a feeling that bravado had already grasped me firmly by the hand.

In the end, my trip around the world took me to 21 countries and carried me hundreds of thousands of miles (I tried to calculate it more accurately several times but gave up!). It was, indeed, a mind-expanding experience and it involved me in some of the most memorable adventures – and misadventures – of my life.

To know what it's like to go backpacking as a middle-aged wannado, is to throw away all thoughts of cosy nights in, or patting dogs, or mowing lawns, or any of those other comforting moments for which many people strive all their working lives. Instead, there comes a clearness of mind, a lifting of burdens, an immediacy of purpose and the heady allure of adventure.

I decided to go it alone because, well, for lots of reasons. It was a tough one. I have always thought of myself as a sharing person – yet here I was, acting with the ultimate selfishness, the maximum indulgence. Maybe that was it in a nutshell; maybe it was time to keep something precious all for myself? Anyway, at least there would be no one to argue with.

Some friends, being kind, looked at my itinerary and assured me the hard part would be the first six months while I was visiting some of the... er, shall we say... less-developed nations. If I survived that and got into the second-half, then the... er, shall we say... civilized world of Australia, New Zealand and North America would be ever such fun. *Quite so.*

Others, being less kind and more practical, warned I would be homesick, or robbed, or set-upon, or worse, and I would get malaria, or syphilis, or AIDS. I would never come back at all, and I would die of malnutrition, or loneliness, or both. *Oh, do you really think so?*

In fact, none of these things happened. True, it was a help that I had kept myself pretty fit. A minor eye infection, a deficiency of something-or-other affecting my fingernails, and stomach problems early on ("India, India," they muttered) – that was the total sum of my ailments. I could have caught a lot worse if I'd stayed at home.

As a globe-trotter, there is a wonderful dual purpose to every new day. First, of course, it is such a privilege to be able to experience so many of the most magical sights and sounds (and even feelings)

ONE WAY or ANOTHER

in the world; but then there is that bit which sets it apart – the *raison d'être*, the yarn from which the holy grail is spun: It is that chance to get up-close with the lifestyles and the customs and the real peoples of those faraway lands; to be, if you are lucky, invited into their homes, to be a part of their lives... and to have the time to do it!

This book is a travelogue in which I have tried to set out a collection of stories and anecdotes and other interesting things that came my way. I've put dates when I wrote them, or when they happened, and while it is true that time will have moved some of them on, the main purpose of this collection is simply to reflect some of the extraordinary, the unusual, and even the bizarre events which are occurring every day in this remarkable world of ours.

There are wonderful, awe-inspiring sights in the world: The jagged Rocky Mountains of North America, the magnificent Himalayas of Nepal, the peace of New Zealand's lakes, the breath-taking panorama of Arizona's Grand Canyon and Death Valley, its surreal near-neighbour, the plunging waters of Niagara and the silky sands of exotic islands in the Pacific and Caribbean ...all of them the most fabulous gifts from nature.

And man-made wonders, too, like the Taj Mahal in India, the Pyramids of Egypt, the golden temples of Thailand and the everlasting CN Tower in Toronto.

Those are the things which pull in tourists by the millions – and I am glad and lucky to have seen them – but, as I said, I

Lake Paringa: One of many wonderful lakes in New Zealand

INTRODUCTION

White-water rafting down the Tulley in Australia

decided not to write the more conventional, serious kind of travel narrative. Instead, this is a collection of eye-witness accounts from an observer and journalist (which was my training) who went, armed with a hankering after the truth, a healthy scepticism of authority, and a wicked sense of humour, on a walk-about tour around the world for a year at a time of life when most people feel safer watching it all on TV.

I wrote as I went, foregoing my laptop in case it got stolen (as it surely would have been) and relying instead on internet cafes, Hotmail folders and the wonderful new world of Mr J. C. R. Licklider. But more of him later... (– see *Shaken by an Economic Earthquake*).

The stories just seemed to happen. I never went looking for them – except to Fiji (*Gunfight in Paradise*) where, in any case, things turned out very differently to what I had envisaged, and – right at the end – to Meredith, a town on the shores of Lake Winnipesaukee in New Hampshire, USA, where I had driven via a customs post across the Canadian border not far away.

"Why do you want to visit America," said the customs man with his stock-standard question.

"I want to visit Meredith," I replied, "and if you look at my name in the passport I think you'll understand why."

"Ah," he said as the penny dropped. "You must be retired. Nothing better to do, eh?"

ONE WAY or ANOTHER

In fact, there had been a great many other things to do: Like following an election in America which will be talked about for years (*Has Anyone Seen the President?*); like witnessing the rioting in Canada's ancient Quebec City when leaders of all the Americas set out plans for globalizing trade (*And The Wall Came Tumbling Down*); and feeling the dot.com bubble bursting in Silicon Valley (*Shaken by an Economic Earthquake*).

Mix in some adventure: Like living with the homeless in San Francisco (*Bums, Aliens and the Urban Poor*), an eight-day safari into the Australian outback (*Throwing Frizbees at the Moon*), and the dangers of white-water rafting (*Taking the Plunge*)... and some misadventure: Like chasing monsters in a country house bedroom in Thailand (*Things That Go Bump in the Night*) and being accused of wearing stolen perfume on a train ride through India (*And the Survey Says*)... and you begin to get the flavour of what a year in the life of a contemporary globe-trotter is all about.

Recently, in Hamilton, a small Canadian city in which I had landed en route from one place to another, I found a travelogue of art spread out among the airport buildings. An abbreviation of the programme notes asserted: "A travelogue is a term first coined in America around 1903, specifically denoting an illustrated lecture (travel + monologue) which seeks to describe the details of one's travels.

"From accounts of short jaunts to extensive diaries of adventures, travelogues are often authored by engaging story-tellers rather than anthropological experts. The travelogue has always been personal; allowing the traveller to equally fill a role of romantic narrator and objective reporter... it offers a historical and cultural insight for those on the move, or simply to aid the poetic goal of 'run-journey-smoother.'"

One Way or Another is the work of a narrator and reporter. If you are travelling, I hope it makes your journey run smoother, and, if you are not, I hope it gets you thinking about what you could be missing.

Richard Meredith
Newport Pagnell, England

ONE WAY ANOTHER

North America

AND THE WALL CAME TUMBLING DOWN

Quebec City, Canada, April 20

I HAD propped myself up with one hand against the fence, head down by my knees, spittle dribbling down my chin. I wanted to vomit but my stomach wouldn't let me. My mouth and nose felt like they were in a microwave and my eyes had lost all focus.

The tap on my shoulder came from a little Japanese guy. "Here, you take water," he said, pulling out a plastic flask from a belt around his waist. He was dressed for battle: Red bandana, soaked in vinegar, pulled over his face, floppy sweatshirt with a rising sun on the front and "fuck the world" on the back, combat-style army trousers, tatty trainers.

I remember thinking: "What the hell are the Japanese doing here in Quebec City?" Then the answer dawned: "Why not? They get everywhere else."

I reached to take the water flask. "No, you no drink – just take and spit," says the little man. I follow instructions. I could tell he knew what he was doing. In it went – a gloriously cooling sensation in my burning mouth. I swill it round and spit. Then my

Teargas and trouble at the Summit

ONE WAY or ANOTHER

eyes. I go to tip the bottle on my searing eyes. "No, no; you no rub," he commands. Again, I do as I am told; you don't feel too good about arguing when you've had a faceful of teargas. Fact is you don't feel too good at all.

I'd had a taste of this weapon of urban warfare years ago in some student demos and marches over union rights. But never anything like this; this is today's product, fit for the millennium. It seems like the whole of central Quebec is enveloped in the stuff, a swirling cloud of nausea which scorches your mouth and scrambles your brain. Word on the street is that this is the version they've sharpened up since Vietnam.

I have just retreated "wounded" from the front line of a major bust-up between protesters and police at the Summit of the Americas, a meeting of the political leaders of 800m people who are here to advocate a partnership between their countries for greater global trade.

The heads of 34 nations from North, Central and South America have gathered for the talks in a convention center not more than 100m away. The only one missing is Fidel Castro from Cuba, who is still in disgrace – at least with George W. Bush, the US President – because of what he did for the Russians and because he doesn't run a democracy.

For the demonstrators outside, this is Big Issue time. In today's world, there is nothing like the topic of globalisation for uniting the dissenting voices of everyone from marxists to ecologists and from those who question every type of human rights to those who suffer every kind of human wrongs.

The clamour against the power of multi-national business, which first erupted into serious violence and disorder in Seattle 17 months ago with the wrecking of a meeting of the World Trade Organisation, is now becoming a din.

Security for the politicians is paramount. They will eat, sleep and talk for three days cocooned in the safety of their modern-day fortress among what is, ironically, an old walled citadel which was breached, only once, when British troops scaled the cliffs of the nearby St Lawrence river nearly 250 years ago.

Today is the summit's opening day. Speeches of welcome are about to begin in the securitised convention center. The world's media knows it. The police guarding the place know it. And those who are outside protesting about it, know it. I can't help

AND THE WALL CAME TUMBLING DOWN

*People not profit:
Demonstrators march on Day 1 of the talks*

wondering, in the tactical nature of these things, who will get their retaliation in first?

The largest security force ever mustered in peacetime Canada has been preparing for this moment. There are said to be 6,000 of them here – local police, riot police, the tough nuts of the *Surete du Quebec*, even the army has detachments on standby. Weeks ago, bemused residents watched as workmen built a fortified wall 10 feet high round their historic Old Quarter. All told, it stretches for about 2.5 miles – a barricade of thick wire mesh atop heavy concrete sections – and it seals off, like Berlin's wall used to, a whole segment of the city center.

The residents were fearful of its consequences when it first went up. And even more so now. The Mayor, Monsieur Jean-Paul L'Allier, a likeable and honest Frenchman, has already apologised to his people for volunteering their city as the venue for this summit. He thought it would be good for trade and business, he said. But that was before the "Battle of Seattle". Now it is a mistake; now it is too late.

ONE WAY or ANOTHER

The balloons go up in protest

The summit has attracted every kind of protest group to Quebec and the wall has attracted huge publicity. Outside of it, right now, are amassing maybe 10,000 demonstrators bent on telling the world that they think the spreading tide of bigger business will lower poorer nations deeper into poverty rather than raise them into riches. It is an argument which leaders in the USA – birthplace of so many of the world's largest corporations – rile against. Wealth creates wealth, they say, it improves performance, raises standards. The issues are profound and fundamental.

Tomorrow there will be 20,000 demonstrators here, and on Sunday still more, but today there is that wall in front of them. To many, it symbolises those very authorities who are right now, over there, planning a future to which they are opposed. The challenge of what to do about it is obvious. But how?

I have walked all around the wall/fence of steel. It seems as secure as a tiger's cage, blocking off the streets and turning the place into a no-go zone. Since its construction, the more creative forces of anti-corporatism have shown their feelings by daubing

AND THE WALL CAME TUMBLING DOWN

some graffiti on the big cement blocks; by fixing up a variety of witty posters and banners to the fence; tying up coloured paper flowers to make it look more like a garden trellis, and by stringing kids balloons along it in a chorus-line of playful indignation.

Nothing very revolutionary there then. But the canny storekeepers know what's coming. Only last night they learned that seven hard cases had been arrested in the city with a *cache* of explosives and weapons which could have done the place some very serious damage.

In the streets near the center, scores of them have been boarding up their shop-fronts. In the ancient rue Saint-Jean, where traders might normally be expecting to serve early visitors in this first weekend of Spring, I notice that McDonald's – proof positive of the scope of global business – has not only closed until further notice, it has taken down its signs and had the shopfront painted over.

Down by the station, in a temporary structure paid for by sympathisers, a "People's Summit" is headquartered as an alternative to the main event. Numbers have been swelling by the hour. Groups are arriving from everywhere – even Japan – summoned by the rallying call of messages on Hotmail and AmericaOnLine. In the tent there is all the paraphernalia of protest: a makeshift auditorium where speakers are dissecting everything from the evils of global power, to racial inequality, the ravages of poverty, worker-exploitation and the plight of polluted whales; a market stall area of tables is laden down with the literature of anti-legislation; the babble of dissatisfaction is all around.

I hear the talk of big bad business. Activists are learning the jargon of mergers and acquisitions, of market domination, monopoly positions and economies of scale. Anti-capitalism is becoming mainstream. *Small is Beautiful*[*] (– see Footnotes) – that banner of the 1970s under which E. F. Schumacker flew the case for alternative economics – has a universal appeal once more. There are broadcasting sound booths in here for an enthusiastic media, and even some rather enterprising types selling souvenirs and badges.

In the streets the atmosphere has taken on a sense of carnival. Here and there are parcels of people making music from guitars and drums. I see a larger group of youngsters dressed like wood elves, singing and dancing in their praise of mother earth. A couple

ONE WAY or ANOTHER

of girls, tall on stilts, chide the penned-in riot cops across the wire. Some middle-aged ladies prance around in fancy dress and large red noses. It almost seems unreal.

They call the troublemakers the Hard Left. Or anarchists. Or radicals. Or dissidents. Or a host of other things, which put a label round those who are prepared to include violence in their agenda for civil confrontation. Some, it must be true, are simply hooligans and thugs. But who's to say that innocence is not now swimming with the tide? The consequences of Big Brotherism are an issue for us all.

I feel the mood changing after a rally near Gate # 1, the main entrance to the walled-in *redoute*. Here, now, is the first major gathering of the clans.

Speaker after speaker climbs up to tell the crowd how globalisation is ruining their lives; how workers are losing their jobs; how families are being made homeless; how the sick are suffering; how pollution is ruining the world. "People Before Profit," the chant goes up, "People Before Profit". It is powerful and emotive. And now, too, I notice sets of people who stand out from the

Confrontation on the front line as the police phalanx holds firm

AND THE WALL CAME TUMBLING DOWN

*The wall is down –
now protesters can savour their moment of victory*

rest. Here is the darker side of democracy; here are those with the labels round them – and the balaclavas, the spiky hair, the nose-studs and the leather jackets. One group I spot are wearing matching facemasks which look like pig snouts. The image is bizarre and threatening.

By chance I am within a stone's throw distance of the drama when it comes.

Out of sight, down the road, I would guess that about 4,000 of the demonstrators have been gathering together for a march up here towards the Gate. It is no coincidence that the time is coming up to 3 o'clock, precisely when the opening speeches inside the convention centre are planned to begin.

And here they come – a chanting, cheering, raucous bunch of humanity that fills the wide avenue like a multi-coloured wave. The police inside the perimeter fence visibly stiffen, form ranks, present their shields, call for re-enforcements to gather on alert.

Close up, the missiles start to fly. Somewhere in the crowd, hidden from view, an arm has hurled a rock. Then another. Now come staves and bits of metal and bags of paint and bleach

ONE WAY or ANOTHER

Officers step forward and fire when they get the command

"bombs" and... oh my God... a plastic bottle with a piece of paper in the top which glows alight and which hits the ground in front of the waiting phalanx to spew out its contents in a cocktail of flame. Soon there is another.

I am near enough to the police for their fear to be palpable. Inside their helmeted uniforms, grotesquely bloated with body armour, I can hear their exclamations and their curses, their words of encouragement to one another and the shouted instructions of their officers to stand steady.

Things are happening fast. Groups of youths – mostly those with the danger labels on – come forward from the pack and climb up onto the wire. In a blink there are dozens of them scaling the fence, reaching back for willing hands which will tug them to and fro'... threading through ropes which have secretly appeared... hauling themselves higher to make the thing top heavy.

Ah, so that's how they mean to do it. Weeks of planning and practice maybe? The authorities got it wrong. They put the wall up too soon. It has given those danger labels the chance to work it out.

AND THE WALL CAME TUMBLING DOWN

But there's no time now for the police to wonder how. The only question is: What should they be doing? The officers survey their troops. The teargas guns are ready. So are the plastic bullets. Young men and women, maybe 200 of them, are strung up on the wire right in front of them like so many rabbits in a shooting gallery; enemies of the State – or are they? – rocking the fence until the concrete blocks beneath start to upend themselves and a whole length of the edifice wobbles in peril.

Indecision runs its course for several long and pregnant seconds. There is no order to fire. The fence is going to fall. Big sections of it are over at crazy angles as it topples, or is being toppled, by the

frenzied crowd. And now a great roar goes up as the first big piece comes tumbling down. The TV cameras zoom in on the action; the world is about to know that it is the rebels of anti-capitalism who have got their retaliation in first.

In all the turmoil it is difficult to make sense of the blurred and tangled picture, but within the briefest time it is clear that the police have decided what to do. Enough is enough. They take several paces backwards, allowing the protesters a moment of victory to jump and jeer on the fallen wall, then they fire their teargas.

One of the hard-core activists, a lad who calls himself Paul and

ONE WAY or ANOTHER

comes from Montreal, tells me later that they had surprised themselves by the speed with which the wall came down. But now that there is a stretch of 50 yards or so at their feet, none of them seems to know quite what to do. Should they fight with the police in the no-man's-land that lies between them? Should they battle through and try to get to the convention centre where (unknown to them) the speeches have been delayed while news of the troubles outside is absorbed? The police, with their volley of teargas, have answered the questions. It is their turn now.

Their strength is considerable. They act like an army. In the first rank, just like infantrymen in those battles of old, are the helmeted "foot soldiers" with batons and riot shields; behind them at every fifth place, men with teargas rifles who step forward and fire when they get the word; and then in the third rank, the anarchists' arch-enemy – men with plastic bullet rifles and stun guns who are using them today, in peace loving Canada, for the very first time.

As a contest, the battle is over. Teargas is impossible to ignore. Its purpose is to disable the ability to function and the first volley gives the police what they want, driving back the main body of the crowd, and sending them fleeing, eyes streaming and hands over mouths, to a safer distance.

It leaves just the veterans, who know about these things, and who have come prepared with gas masks of their own, padding beneath their clothes, and vinegar or apple cider in their scarves, as an isolated group beside the wire-mesh debris of their triumph.

For half-an-hour the hard-core stand there in defiance. They have red flags and accents which give them away as Canadians. It is as if their national pride should set them at the front.

"You don't want to be here. We don't want to be here. We are citizens, we have rights. Why don't you let us through?" shouts the burly, bearded leader.

"Who's got the weapons? Who's got the guns?" screams the girl beside him. "We have nothing." And she spreads her arms out wide in evidence.

Others are joining in, taunting the police ranged up before them. "Why are you doing this? Why are you protecting those people? What are you doing with our democracy, our freedom of speech?"

At length, the police have heard enough. The phalanx of foot

AND THE WALL CAME TUMBLING DOWN

A wounded demonstrator is arrested and led away

soldiers moves forward, beating their Plexiglas shields with batons in a rhythm of intimidation. It's all over bar the shouting.

A few swearings and scuffles, but now, inevitably, there can only be ritual resistance and the first arrests are made.

That night, workmen busy themselves repairing the wall, the security forces bring in all their reinforcements, and not once more, despite their growing weight of numbers, do the protesters manage to break through the massed ranks of police defenders.

Capitalism goes back to its big business; the politicians go back to their people; the protesters go back to their grievances. In gentle Canada – one of the most tolerant and civilised of nations – maybe they fixed it that everyone could leave Quebec with some kind of victory. *Je me souviens*, says the slogan of the province... "I will remember." There can be little doubt of that.

ONE WAY or ANOTHER

Footnotes:

1. The summit nations, whose economies account for a combined $11 trillion in annual GDP, agreed to move further towards their "free trade" partnership and set a deadline for it to begin in 2005. Measures include lowering trade barriers and cutting cross-border red tape for business.

2. Over the Quebec weekend, there were 400 arrests and more than 120 people were hurt including several policemen. Some of the worst violence came on Saturday when police enforced their efforts to protect the security zone with water cannons and "flash" grenades. Rioters lit fires, which went out of control, damaged property and smashed car windows. But many more marched peacefully in another part of town.

3. Less than two weeks later, an estimated crowd of 5,000 staged an anti-globalisation rally in Oxford Street, London. There were 50 arrests and 11 people were taken to hospital.

4. E. F. Schumacher's book *Small is Beautiful** – "a study of economics as if people mattered" – was first published in 1973. The German-born Dr Schumacher studied economics at Oxford in the 1930s and later taught it at Columbia University, New York. He was economic advisor to the British Control Commission in Germany after World War II and was one of the first to question whether multi-national companies were good for us or our planet. He proposed instead, smaller working units, communal ownership and regional workplaces utilizing local labour. Capital should serve Man, he argued, not the other way round.

5. A Canadian, John Peters Humphrey, former law professor at McGill University, is credited with authoring the Universal Declaration of Human Rights, adopted by the United Nations in 1948.

© Richard Meredith & Mercury Books – all rights reserved

STILL ON TRACK

Canada; March

THE railway that crosses Canada coast to coast has a history and a symbolism that is second to none.

It is a thread of steel which binds together the second largest country on the planet (Russia, despite all its recent upheavals, is still the biggest).

It is – in a land where there are more telegraph poles than people – often the only way that folk in some of the world's most remote areas can get to see their relatives and friends or buy the groceries.

More controversially, it is – as some political analysts tell us – the only reason why Canada is not part of the United States. It is also – as history tells us – a fountain of stories involving double-dealing, intrigue and general chicanery.

Its passengers have included British Royalty, film stars, explorers,

The Canadian pulls out of Toronto on its three-day journey across the country. It is one of the great train journeys of the world

ONE WAY or ANOTHER

prime ministers and men in beaverskin hats from the backwoods of nowhere. And it runs on time (or 2 minutes early for a 72-hour journey if you really want to be precise).

When Canadian Pacific, a private company, was given the job of completing the trans-continental railway in 1881, it was on a hiding to nothing. The government had given up on its own efforts; others had tried, and failed. The task was to connect up existing track by building "missing links" across boggy muskeg land above Lake Superior and to go up over the Rocky Mountains in the west where the acquisitive Americans were looking to move in.

Sir John Macdonald, the nation's first Prime Minister and a loquacious, charismatic Scot who sometimes took more port than both his legs would stand, resigned amidst a financial scandal involving the funding of the company. And worse... mandated by HM's government in London to 'Confederate' the provinces of its vast North American colony, he had only been able to win British Columbia's agreement to join up with a promise that they would be connected to everyone else by the railway within 10 years.

It was a promise – which in those days anyway – the politicians felt duty-bound to keep.

Swathed in hardship, frostbite and tales of daring-do, thousands of labourers (mostly Irish and Chinese) toiled to dig and dynamite

Snaking through the forested lower peaks of the Caribou range

STILL ON TRACK

Enthusiastic crowds greeted the first train into Vancouver. It was decorated with banners, greenery and a portrait of Queen Victoria
PHOTO COURTESY OF CANADIAN PACIFIC

their way through the Rockies after surveyors had searched for months to map out a route.

In parts of Ontario, a land of quick-sinking muskegs, frustrated tracklayers often awoke to find their efforts of the day before simply vanished overnight into the gooey depths of a shifting bog.

Despite it all, such was the national pride and importance of the project, the work was nonetheless completed, not in the promised 10 years, but in just 4½. And the first passenger train ran coast-to-coast six months later.

Today, symptomatic of the new era of privatisation, the transcontinental is run by an outfit called Via, which rents the track from Canadian National Railways (CN).

With connections, it is possible to travel the full 4,200 miles coast-to-coast from Halifax in the east to Prince Rupert in the west, and Via's smart, stainless steel "Canadian" – which proudly carries the legend Train #1 – is one of THE great train journeys of the world. It covers the 3,000 miles between Toronto and

ONE WAY or ANOTHER

**John and Yoko
Give Peace a Chance in the Queen Elizabeth hotel**
PHOTO: COURTESY OF CANADIAN PACIFIC

Vancouver and runs three times a week. Main halts in between are Sudbury, Winnipeg, Saskatoon, Edmonton, Jasper and Kamloops although, remarkably, it will also make request stops for passengers – even singletons – to get on or off at one-moose towns in the back of beyond.

When Canadian Pacific's first passenger train hissed and puffed its way across the country and into history in 1886 it took nearly 6 days. Now it takes half that time to trundle across the vast wateriness of Ontario, the glaciated fur-trading lands of Manitoba, the wheatfield prairies of Saskatchewan and the cattle ranches of Alberta.

In the Rockies, the line follows much of the original path through the Yellowhead Pass with spectacular views of snowy

STILL ON TRACK

mountain tops and icy rivers, before snaking down into British Columbia through the forested lower peaks of the Caribou, Monashee and Columbia ranges.

Although it has mostly back-tracked out of railways since the 1960s, Canadian Pacific is one of the wealthiest companies in Canada. Its name is practically an institution and its history is entwined like ivy round the progress of the nation.

At one time or another it has owned more than 36 million acres of the place (that's roughly equivalent to the size of England and Wales combined) and part of its brief in those early days was to act more like a government development agency in bringing out settlers to the now-prosperous west coast. It even gave away farmland in exchange for wages to contractors who worked on the railway.

Over the years CP's tentacles have stretched by vertical integration into most things connected with travel, shipping and freight.

Today, probably its most public face is through the chain of Canadian hotels – all sumptuous and picturesque – which it owns in places like Quebec City (Chateau Frontenac), the Rockies (Chateau Lake Louise), Toronto (Royal York), Ottawa (Chateau Laurier), Victoria (Empress) and the Hotel Vancouver.

Guests have included royalty, heads of state from far and yon, and the rich and famous. John Lennon, the late Beatle, recorded *Give Peace a Chance* between the sheets with Yoko Ono in suite 1742 at the Queen Elizabeth hotel in Montreal during his week-long anti-Vietnam bed-in protest in 1969. (You can still hire it for just Can $599 a night).

Through its purchase of control of the Fairmont chain, CP's hotel collection now also stretches into Mexico, the Caribbean and throughout the USA.

The company's original "Mr Hotels" was Charles Melville Hays who had previously built up the Grand Trunk Pacific Railroad and then sold it to them. A former US citizen who moved to Canada, he was on his way back there in 1912 aboard the *Titanic* when ... well, he didn't make it.

In fact CP had a difficult time with boats. Around the turn of the century they accumulated big fleets of passenger liners and coastal freighters, but disaster struck in 1914 when their *Empress of Ireland* collided with a collier in fog in the Gulf of St Lawrence. The boat sank in just 14 minutes and the dead totalled 1,012 passengers and crew – almost as many as the *Lusitania* and not far

ONE WAY or ANOTHER

Journey's end:
The Canadian arrives at Pacific Central Station, Vancouver –
two minutes early after three days

short of the *Titanic's* awful toll.

Four years later, there was another horror when all 360 aboard their coaster *Princess Sophia* perished after it hit a reef in a snowstorm off Alaska.

Like its passenger trains, CP pretty much bailed out of passenger boats in the 1960s and now makes its money from hotels, cargo ships, fuel, rail freight and running luxury train tours (*a la* the Orient Express) round bits of the old trans-continental track it still owns at prices in the O-O-O gauge.

Further reading:

The Great Railway by Pierre Berton (McClelland & Stewart Inc.)
Canadian Pacific by John Lorne McDougall (McGill University Press).

© Richard Meredith & Mercury Books – all rights reserved

HAS ANYONE SEEN THE PRESIDENT?

Chapter 1
It's a hell of a job

USA; February

THE Smithsonian Institute in Washington is a kind of super depository of all things historically American.

Stretched across town are buildings on 16 separate sites packed with all the treasures and trappings of people who have plotted the path of this extraordinary nation.

The world and his wife come to visit. It is, we are told, the largest collection of museums, galleries, research and educational establishments on earth. There are more branches elsewhere in America and overseas. In short, it's one of the very best places to go if you want to know what's been happening round here.

Interestingly, I discover that the money to start it all came from a diminutive scientist of questionable English parentage who never actually crossed the Atlantic. But that's another story and it will have to wait. (– see *Up Yours Dad! in PASSING THOUGHTS...*)

Truth to tell, I am visiting the Institute for only one reason: They are staging a special exhibition called "The American Presidency" and, as subjects go, it's about the hottest topic in the universe just now.

Washington, of course, is a natural for an exhibition like this. Nowhere in America is more presidential. Just down the road from where I am, is the White House, which every president except the first (George Washington) has called his home.

Then, up on the hill, is the Capitol building, the domed, strikingly-imposing House of Congress, where the nation's politicians work out how to run this place. Or, since the president has the power to veto or approve anything they do, perhaps we should say *'help him to run this place'*.

Everywhere there are more examples of the huge responsibilities vested in this nation's leader: The austere Pentagon building

ONE WAY or ANOTHER

The Smithsonian: America's super-depository of history

where those who run America's armed forces, answer to his control; the J.Edgar Hoover building which houses his top policemen; all the big departments of state; all the civil servants; all those secret service people down the road at Langley...

The president is, as the exhibition soon reminds me, a uniquely powerful person: America's First Citizen, its Chief Executive, Leader of the Nation, Commander of the Armed Forces, its top Diplomat, Manager of the Economy... it's an awesome task.

Former presidents have come up with their own descriptions. John F.Kennedy called it "this glorious burden"; Harry S. Truman found it "like riding a tiger"; Thomas Jefferson thought it a "splendid misery"; Warren G. Harding fired straight from the hip: "It's a hell of a job," he said.

The exhibition is absorbing. 200 years and then-some of relics, reminders and reminiscences of those who have held America's ultimate public office.

Artifacts range from the mundane to the remarkable. Here, apparently, is the blood of Abraham Lincoln on the lace cuff of a lady theatergoer who comforted him as he lay dying from an assassin's bullet; here the bear which gave Theodore 'teddy'

Roosevelt his nickname; here the table-top radio mike through which Franklin Roosevelt encouraged the nation to greater efforts in World War II.

There is much from modern presidents, too. Here some flickering, black and white pictures of that terrible day in Dallas when JFK was shot; here a battered filing cabinet from the Watergate affair which led to the downfall and disgrace of Richard Nixon; here a cowboy hat from actor-President Ronald Reagan; here a saxophone from Bill Clinton... and film of the House impeaching him for lying about Monica Lewinski.

Ah, but now this is odd. Where, I wonder, is all the stuff of victory from the election of George W. Bush, America's latest and 43rd holder of the presidential office? I check again. No, there simply isn't a thing. Not a sticker. Not a photograph. Not so much as an empty champagne glass. "We just haven't managed to catch up with it all," said the busybusy lady at the inquiry desk when I asked.

I know what she means. It's been three months now since the son of George Bush Snr, the 41st president, got into power. But even the Smithsonian, one of the world's greatest keepers of record, hasn't put up a hook to hang his hat on.

Harry Houdini, the legendary escapologist, would have been a good stand-in.

America and its presidency has never known an election trauma quite like it. George Bush Jnr is getting on with the business of running the country. But millions of Americans are still not sure why.

It's a long and complicated story, but I'll try to tell you what happened.

Chapter 2
Oops, I'll read that again

Monday, February 19

It seems appropriate that I should be writing this today. It's President's Day. In the beginning it was decreed as a public holiday to mark George Washington's birthday. Then they combined it with Abraham Lincoln's which was around the same time. Now they just call it on the third Monday in February to "remember

ONE WAY or ANOTHER

George W. Bush: 43rd president

the achievements of all America's presidents." Most of the nation has taken the day off. I imagine George W. Bush, the new president, is having a rest-day, too. I'm sure he can do with it.

There have been just over 100 days since November 7, the day the record books will show he was elected. In some countries the First 100 Days is called a honeymoon period for a new administration. For many Americans, it's been more like a nightmare.

In fact, millions of words have been written and said about this president's election and what has happened since.

Even today I am told that at least nine books are already under way and there are official inquiries in progress on everything from the performance of TV commentators to the standard of ballot papers.

The whole of America's system of democracy is under question. It's as big as that. I make no apologies for writing about it, too. Of all the things which have happened on this journey of mine around the world, this is the least expected – but without doubt the most important. And, as luck would have it, I have been here through it all.

I liked these words from Norman Ornstein, a senior resident scholar at the American Enterprise Institute, who wrote the other day: "Here was an election in which Americans learned, as vividly as one can imagine, that every vote really does count. Unfortunately, they also learned that not every vote is counted – not even close."

He added: "For those of us who study elections, the sloppy, sometimes incompetent and occasionally corrupt administration (of them) – in a process more de-centralised than anything other than garbage collection – has been a fact of life. For everybody else, it is a shock..."

And yes, it has been a shock. An alarming surprise and a great disappointment. A mixture of emotions ranging from the pain of a shattered illusion to the feeling you get when a rock gets turned over in a place full of worms.

HAS ANYONE SEEN THE PRESIDENT?

The first big surprise comes with the discovery of what they call in America the "popular vote."

This is a young country. Not much more than a couple of centuries ago it was full of wild frontiersmen. At the Smithsonian, they tell how the early presidents were led into leadership at the head of torch-light parades.

These days there are campaign trails and bandwagons and TV pundits and billions of dollars spent on hype. The method is different but the illusion the same. It seems like whoever is ahead in the popularity polls gets the job in the White House. Even the pedestrian Smithsonian calls the bandwagon process "a massive expression of the nation's will."

But that's as maybe. For in this latest election for president, as we now know, defining the "will of the people" is a science which is light years away from being exact.

For one thing, a large number of people don't get to voice their opinion at all. They are the estimated 3 million, mostly Hispanics or Black Afro-Americans, who do not appear on the national 10-year census. They are the citizens of Nowhere Townsville.

Then there is the huge number of 60 million Americans –

Al Gore with running mate Dan Lieberman. He polled more votes- but still lost the closest election in presidential history

ONE WAY or ANOTHER

about half of the total electorate – who don't actually think it worth voting. Period.

Even the "popular vote" (which actually means the candidate who gets the most) isn't the decider. Again, as we now know, the Democrat Al Gore polled 530,000 more votes in this election than George Bush, his Republican opponent, but he still lost.

It hasn't happened like that for over 100 years. But it's happened now.

So how did George W. Bush ever get to be president? It's a question which has been taxing me, most of America, and a large proportion of the world's population.

And the answer, it seems – after an experience which the American public will never forget – is partly because their system can actually allow for such a thing to happen; and partly, let's be honest, because of that wormy mess which gets found under rocks.

The first is only slightly less of a shock and a disappointment than the second.

As you've heard from Norman Ornstein, the American process of electing presidents is incredibly de-centralised. It is also full of twists and turns. As a matter of fact, most Americans I've talked to don't actually understand it. But I'll have a try at explaining.

The President is the Head of State and Chief Executive of government. As such, he (and I can say that because there hasn't been a she. Yet.) must be able to count on the majority support of the legislature. Just one more supporter than the other side is, quite literally, enough. And that's what it all came down to in this historic election.

Congress (otherwise known as parliament) has two sets of politicians who meet to debate and decide on legislation in that wonderful Capitol building in Washington. They are the Senate, with 100 members, and the House of Representatives, which has 435.

The Senators and the Representatives are sent to Congress by the 50 States within the Union – two from each for the Senate and a variable number from each (it depends on population size) to the House.

On this election day of November 7, when it comes right down to the wire, it is the voters of Florida (or, to be absolutely clear, *'those who actually voted in Florida'*) who hold the keys to the White House.

Tuesday, November 7; election night

Torchlight parades are a thing of the past. So now, as usual, we are given the message on TV. As day turns into evening, we are told by increasingly breathless sets of commentators that declarations of support in every state have left the result virtually neck-and-neck between Messrs Bush and Gore.

It really is a close one. Whoever wins the... er... popular vote in Florida, we hear, gets all of the state's allocation of 25 Representatives, and with them, the presidency.

Quick, let's get over to the vote-count in Florida.

At 7.52pm precisely, we get the result. You know the kind of thing: "They are still voting in Florida (as indeed they are in several other places) but all the surveys and exit polls and projections show... "Yes, Gore has won Florida. And with it, the Presidency."

Hallelujah! Or words to that effect if you are a supporter of the Democratic party; something probably unmentionable, if you are not.

Turn to the other channels and, yes, you can sense them getting that new display case ready in the Smithsonian.

But TV's messengers of the gods are wrong. Humbled. Embarrassed. And wrong. All of those experts and pundits and analysts, with all of their charts and graphs and computer predictions, have jumped too soon.

Around 15 million people live in Florida, although, as we've heard, less than half of them actually vote. They divide into 67 counties. The result takes some piecing together, but around midnight it looks official: Bush, and not Gore, has won. The margin is just 930 votes.

Or is it? Nerves are getting a little frayed on the TV. "It's too close to call," we are told. "There will be a recount in Florida."

Ah, so it's not all over yet then.

Chapter 3
Worms under the rock

A lot of things happen when really big cheeses come down to the wire. First of all, the atmosphere gets very serious; second of all, things which wouldn't have mattered much before, now become

ONE WAY or ANOTHER

very important; third of all, people start asking awkward questions. Questions like: "Can it be true that just a handful of votes will stop me from becoming President of the United States of America and Leader of the Western World?"

Wednesday, November 8

Yesterday America should have had a president. Today they are not sure who. So, as the rules say when the voting is as close as it appears to be in Florida, they need to start checking things out again.

In the Sunshine State the atmosphere is about to get serious, everything is going to matter a lot, and some very awkward questions will be asked. The whole of America – and most of the world, it seems – wants to find out what's going on.

For those who don't know, Tallahassee is Florida's capital city, although quite why it earned that right I'm not altogether sure. One version I've heard, is that it was only chosen because it fell halfway between everywhere else that mattered in the state. But that's probably cruel. My own conclusion is that it must have been because it's so tidy.

In England it would be a garden city, like Letchworth or Welwyn. It is quite smugly neat and tidy; the kind of town where a tree might get arrested for dropping a leaf in the wrong place.

Half of the buildings belong to the omnivorous Florida State University, the rest to officialdom. On the hilltop in the centre of town is a *coterie* of glass and concrete – the county (Leon) courthouse, the civic centre, the cultural centre and the supreme court... all conveniently close to each other and all over-shadowed, quite literally, by Capitol Tower, a monolithic 22-storey office block housing the state's politicians and administrators, which sticks up from the middle like a suburban lighthouse.

Katherine Harris, who is Florida's

Capitol Tower: A suburban lighthouse in the city centre

HAS ANYONE SEEN THE PRESIDENT?

George W's brother Jeb

Katherine Harris

Secretary of State and ultimately in charge of running their elections, works from here. So does Jeb Bush, brother of the man who is at this very moment nearly, but not quite, certain of being the next exhibit in a display case at the Smithsonian. He is State Governor; the top man. His office is cheek-by-jowl with Mrs Harris's on the ground floor of Capitol Tower. They are both leading Republicans. Together, they have been championing the Bush-for-President campaign in these parts. I imply nothing improper, but if I was a supporter of their party, I'm sure I would think it... er... rather convenient, shall we say, to have them both here just now.

Anyway, this is the place, and these are the people, on whom the spotlight of fame is about to fall.

First into town, as you might expect, is the news media – that tough-skinned and inquisitive bunch who are always on hand when big cheeses get close to the wire. In no time at all, hundreds

Together: Jeb Bush and Mrs Harris's offices are only yards apart

ONE WAY or ANOTHER

of journalists, photographers and camera crews are jostling about. The streets are full of mobile TV studios with those neat little dishes on top. There's no room at the inns.

Next come the lawyers. Not that there aren't more than a few in town already; what with all the big courts being here like I've said. But this is the presidency don't forget. We aren't exactly talking parking violations, OK?

Both sides are hiring the best advice. Barely 24 hours have passed since election day but the legal heavy-weights are heading here faster than the field in the Kentucky Derby and if you suspect that some of us have already concluded that this recount business will be no simple exercise in maths, you would not be wrong.

The reason is this: When lawyers get involved in things over here (and when don't they?) nothing goes easy. Then there's the fact that the law and politics are all mixed up on this side of the Atlantic. It makes for a double-whammy of tortuous proportions.

In America you see, it is never an offence to announce your political persuasion. Quite the reverse in fact – it's expected; even if you are a judge.

For most of the time I don't suppose it matters much if one half of someone happens to be chairman of the Young Tiddlypushers Party while the other half is serving salami sandwiches at the local deli.

However, if he/she happens to be a judge and his/her court is about to be asked to make rulings which could deliver the next presidency, well that's rather different

All votes are equal, as we know, but some votes are more equal than others. In Florida, I discover, senior judges in the state's Supreme Court have been noted for giving rulings along party lines. The majority of them are Democrats. In Washington, the federal supreme court's judges are said to Conservatives (whatever that means). These are points to bear in mind when things hot up a little later, if you get my drift.

Anyway, back at the recount, the issue seems to be as deceptively simple as a Rubik cube. The challenge for Mr Gore is to persuade the court that he's entitled to more votes than he got first time around; while Mr Bush will argue that he isn't. But you know what lawyers are.

At one time or another, every court and every judge in

HAS ANYONE SEEN THE PRESIDENT?

Tallahassee is involved. The circuit court, the county court, the state court, appeals court, supreme court ... there are hearings, and judgements, and appeals to judgements. Up and down we go; round and round we go. It's the Full Monty. Mr Gore, as you would expect, wants to do some serious homework on the way Florida has been keeping the score. He wants all those rocks upturned. Underneath, it's not a pretty sight.

America is agog at some of the evidence which comes to light.

Like Norman Ornstein said, the election process is hugely decentralised. In the Sunshine State, as with every other, the local administration is left to get on with things. County supervisors, underpaid and under-trained, make their own decisions about what to spend on counting equipment, who to hire, even how the ballot forms should look.

Courts hear that the system is a mess – a hotch-potch of voting machinery, much of it old and inaccurate; an assortment of ballot forms, some incredibly user-unfriendly; and a voting public which is often uneducated in what to do and with no help to guide them.

Forgive me, if you will, for leaving aside some of the questions about whether anyone was actually prevented from voting (a claim about which several civil rights groups are currently suing the state)... Allow me, also, the benefit of not having to recall whether the ballots of absentee voters which got delayed in the post, were finally included or not (I'm honestly not sure if the courts ever did decide on that one)...

Here are some examples of what was said in court:

Uncontested evidence is given that up to 60 per cent of the voters in Florida used punch-card machines which are more than 20 years old.

Voters encounter a variety of problems. Some say the machines won't line up correctly on the names or numbers they want; others find the machines don't punch out holes completely, leaving the "chad" dangling like a piece of torn skin; or not punching out a hole at all, but leaving instead a dimpled mark on the paper as if it had wanted to but changed its mind.

New phrases enter the language. "Hanging chads", "pregnant chads", "dimpled chads" and sundry other kinds of electoral anatomy become the stuff of bar-room debate from Sacramento to Sarasota.

Election administrators, we are told, try to puzzle out the

ONE WAY or ANOTHER

answers for themselves. In one district they even tape "hanging chads" back in place, being convinced that these voters have changed their minds in midpunch, so to speak. Another expression – "determining voter intention" – enters the dictionary for these queried ballots. There are, apparently, 60,000 of them.

Voting Guide: Florida-style

"It all comes down to a lack of money," one tally supervisor tells a judge. "If there's a choice between spending money on roads or schools or a new voting machine which might only be used once or twice a year, what would you do?"

Then there are the ballot papers.

With no standard format, local election officers are free to design their own. Many of them do.

The main idea of the General Election, of course, is to select the president and his deputy from a list of candidates. Sounds easy. But, as with everything else in this convoluted American system, it isn't. Other elections, for several statewide political and judicial positions, are balloted at the same time. They even use the opportunity to ask what people think about some local issues. I guess the theory is that combining it all together will save time.

Anyway, the net result is too much for some folk to understand. Helpful supervisors try their best, we are told. They list names out alphabetically, for example, or arrange them in different political groups on separate pages ("butterfly votes" – another new phrase). But, oh dear, some people are never much good with names...

In one famous instance, Mr Bush is found to have been paired with Monica Moorehead, an Afro-American atheist representing a New York based party standing for the "revolutionary struggle of workers and all oppressed people against this rotten capitalist system."

It is not hard to get confused enough to spoil your vote. In fact, the courts hear, there's a whole bunch of ways.

HAS ANYONE SEEN THE PRESIDENT?

The result? 145,000 ballots are voided-out across the voting booths of Florida.

Gore concentrated his fire-power on counties with the most disputed votes

ONE WAY or ANOTHER

Nonsensically, while some counties have allowed certain types of voter error, others, faced with the same problem, have not.

When all is said and done, Florida has more than 200,000 votes in the disallowed, spoiled or disputed categories. It's a whole heap of worms.

Sunday, November 26

When it comes, 19 days after the original election day, the outcome of the recount is a huge disappointment to the Gore camp – and a travesty of justice according to his supporters.

Legal argy-bargy takes time; caseloads of it. The nation is rudderless, the people are getting impatient. It cannot go on for ever. Mrs Harris sets a deadline.

Florida's supreme court (that's the one with the majority of Democrat judges, remember?) votes to allow the worms – those 200,000 disallowed, spoiled or disputed ballots – to get an individual inspection (a manual recount) to determine "voter intention". But, oh heavens, there is hardly any time left.

Illegal votes: One of many election problems at Florida's polls

HAS ANYONE SEEN THE PRESIDENT?

Florida's Supreme Court in Tallahassee

The recount result is startling. In Miami/Dade and Palm Beach, two of Florida's most-populated counties – and which turned in most of the voting queries – both fail to meet the deadline and nothing gets changed at all. They ask for more time, but Mrs Harris refuses. It's her prerogative, by all accounts.

Another surprise and disappointment is also in store for the Democrats. Of the other 65 counties, only 16 have come up with any amendments to their original figures.

Total votes are now 2,912,790 for Bush against 2,912,253 for Gore, a net swing of only 393 votes from the first count and enough to give Bush an "official" victory in the state by just 537 votes out of a total of nearly 6 million.

Puzzlingly, it very much appears that Bush has triumphed by an... er... popular vote. But whichever way you look at it, he has won in an epic election escape that Harry Houdini would have been proud to perform.

Mrs Harris, looking relieved and excited, appears on TV to certify the result: Florida has spoken, Mr Bush is to be the next president after all.

But it still isn't over.

Chapter 4
Close, but no cigar

America is stunned by the revelations in court. Newspaper editorials have been full of words like farce and shambles, debacle, disgrace and disaster. On TV, satirists and comedians are having a field day. The two contestants have become Mr Dumb and Mr Dumber; Bush's middle name initial is re-styled "Dubya", mimicking his laconic southern drawl and to avoid confusion with his father, George Bush Snr, the former president who claims, I believe, to be a distant relative of Britain's present Queen; Mrs Harris is lampooned as the "brassy lassie from Tallahassee". Harry H is turning in his grave.

More seriously, critics have dug up the fact that America spends five times as much on helping organizations like the UN to monitor the fairness of elections in Third World countries as they do on the organisation of their own. It helps to explain a few things, but no one seems to have the courage to ask the UN if they would have approved of this one.

In brief, these are not the kind of circumstances which normally greet a new Leader of the Western World.

The Gore camp consults the rule-book. Never before has a presidential election result been challenged after a recount decision – but his lawyers tell him there's no reason why he shouldn't. What he wants is simple (that word again); he wants a proper hand-count of Florida's disputed ballots because he is sure there will be enough in his favour to overturn Bush's tiny majority. What he needs is an independent assessment of what those voters really intended.

So back we go to court again. Back come the journalists, back come those TV vans with the neat little dishes on top, back come the lawyers and the judges.

Gore's team tactics are to concentrate on the disputed votes of three counties – Miami/Dade, Palm Beach and Broward. The reason is that all three are in south-east Florida where the majority of people live; all have high minority group populations (who traditionally vote Democrat); and because together they account for most of the disputed ballots.

But persuading the courts to agree how it should be done is, as usual, quite another matter.

HAS ANYONE SEEN THE PRESIDENT?

It is practically a re-run. Back and forth go the arguments. Who's going to do the "assessing"? Who's going to agree or disagree their decisions? When is a dimple more like a pimple? When is a butterfly more like a moth? At one stage, a circuit court judge orders more than a million votes to be brought to him in Tallahassee so he can have a look at them for himself.

They are driven up-State in a convoy of trucks under police escort. It all takes time.

And now there is another deadline looming: December 12 – the day when the "electoral college" (parliament) must be convened; a date which is fixed by the rule book. The days tick by; still no definitive legal ruling.

The supreme court in Washington: Held emergency sessions

Friday, December 8

At last we again reach the top of the local pile. Florida's Supreme Court makes up its mind. The vote is 4:3. Yes, they will allow a hand-count of disputed ballots in ALL counties, including the three that Gore wants most. There are four days to go... the weekend is coming... election staff have been counting themselves to sleep with votes instead of sheep for weeks... But this is for the presidency, this is for democracy, this is for the western world.

The tellers go to work again. The Gore camp is high on expectation. The nation holds its breath.

ONE WAY or ANOTHER

Saturday, December 9

But wait. There's still time for yet another twist in this dramatic and convoluted saga. The federal supreme court in Washington – the nation's highest court and the only place now capable of trumping anything those judges in Florida have said – is in emergency session at the request of Bush's team.

Normally, these... er... Conservative judges don't interfere in the decisions of state courts. They've gone on record for saying as much. But nothing is normal about this election, like everybody knows.

It's 3.10pm in Florida when the word comes through from Washington. The two-sentence edict is read out on the steps of the courthouse in Tallahassee. Folk gathered round might easily have expected someone to shout "Oh yez, oh yez" and ring a bell. It was like a national proclamation, and the sense of the announcement went something like this: "Hold everything! We want to have a think about what's happening..."

In Leon county, the supervisor reckoned they were just 10 minutes away from finishing the job; Broward, Miami/Dade and Palm Beach were not much more behind. But the election officials did what they were told. They stopped what they were doing and went home to enjoy the rest of the weekend.

Monday, December 11 (late)

A puff of smoke comes out from the courthouse on Washington's Capitol Hill. "No," say the judges there by 5:4, "there will be no manual count after all."

Why? Well, there were pages of reasons. So many, in fact, that most experts I listened to or read opinions from, couldn't actually fathom out what the main ones were. Let's just say that the judges ruled the exercise unconstitutional.

Tuesday, December 12

Whatever the legal interpretation, the decision by the judges in Washington, effectively brings to an end this most extraordinary, most disturbing, and most dramatic of elections.

That 537-vote recount majority for Bush must stand. Gore concedes defeat, the "electoral college" goes ahead as a formality, and Bush can finally call himself president-elect.

It is exactly 35 days since General Election Day; a five-week roller-coaster ride in which the most powerful nation on the planet has been covered in embarrassment and confusion as the dirty linen of its democratic process has been washed out for all to see.

Chapter 5
Wearing the hair-shirt

As I say, I am writing this in February on President's Day. Between now and all that drama in December there has been the big inauguration in Washington for the swearing in of Mr Bush as President.

The contrast of moods was obvious. In the nation's capital, Republicans partied late into the previous night to celebrate their return to power; on the day there was all the pomp and ceremony that goes with one of the nation's great events; in

Capitol Hill: Scene of the inauguration

ONE WAY or ANOTHER

Tallahassee 1,000 civil rights and union leaders marched in protest, saying they were "returning to the scene of the crime."

I have been spending some time talking to the people of Miami/Dade and the counties adjacent to it – Broward and Palm Beach – along the eastern seaboard.

A mind-boggling place, Miami. Chaotic might be the best word to describe it. A city of 2m people – easily the biggest in Florida – and that's not counting the torrent of folk passing through, either via the airport (one of the main connecting "hubs" in America), or by land on their way south to the Keys, or north to Jacksonville and Orlando, or by sea.

It's a huge amalgam of races and customs and conflicting lifestyles. Along the sands of South Beach and Miami Beach, and Coconut Grove and Key Biscayne, film idols and rock stars mingle with the crowds. Here live, or have lived, the likes of Sylvester Stallone, Arnold Schwarzenegger, Madonna, Cher and Sharon Stone. Here, one of the fashion world's biggest names – Gianni Versace – was famously murdered outside his mansion.

It is a place where the beautiful people come to see and be seen. But it is also a city with a record through the 1970s and '80s of race riots and gang warfare.

There are drugs and clubs and sleazy sex parlours. To the north-west lies the suburb of Liberty City, an inaptly-named place of deep urban deprivation; to the south-west Little Havana. Spanish is a common language everywhere and nearly half of all minority groups have origins in nearby Cuba, whose "freedom flights" to America after the missile crisis in JFK's time delivered hundreds of thousands of refugees.

Interestingly, I find that Jeb Bush, the President's brother, has many connections with the city. For a time, in the 1980s, he ran a real estate company here; his family lived locally, and his three children all went to school here.

In America, where glad-handing and personal contacts are such an important part of politics, I can't help thinking it will have been... er... useful for a would-be president to have a brother with such good connections in a place which ultimately had such a pivotal role in his election.

I also find that Miami had the unfortunate distinction only two years ago of having its mayor removed from office after a vote-rigging scandal.

Regrettably, at his office in Tallahassee, where I am anxious to put these and other observations to Jeb Bush, I find I am about as welcome as an elephant with wind.

Mrs Harris, on the other hand, is attracted to the thought of an article comparing her with Britain's Mrs Thatcher. I ask to see her at the mansion in town she has converted in a style which befits this will-be heiress of a $6.5m fortune from her citrus-farming grand-father. But, what bad luck, she is just off on a trade mission to promote Florida's benefits to, ironically, the UK.

Elsewhere, the new powers-that-be have donned a collective hairshirt in their efforts to put right what went wrong with the election, and a host of official and unofficial inquirers is out and about inspecting stable doors; the most important of them being:

- An assessment by experts into the cost of upgrading and/or replacing all out-dated voting equipment, probably with optical, touch-screen machines;
- Independent investigations by several media consortia into the "voter intentions" of Florida's pile of disputed votes;
- An analysis of the benefits of introducing a ballot paper of uniform design and standard;
- An inquiry into the quality, selection and training of election supervisors and their staffs, and the merits of a voter-education programme;
- A legal claim by civil rights groups that some blacks were physically deterred from voting and that help was denied non-English-speaking minorities.

TV executives, already roasted by a senate committee, have recommended all polling booths close at the same time wherever they are, and have agreed not to "call" an election result in future until all votes are in.

They are still smarting from a report on election night coverage which accused them of "staging a collective drag race to be first with the news" and of "recklessly endangering the electoral process... for commercially questionable reasons."

And what of the central characters in this extraordinary political saga?

ONE WAY or ANOTHER

Al Gore, who was once a newspaper reporter, has taken a job as a visiting professor to the School of Journalism at Columbia University, New York. Bill Clinton, the outgoing president who originally defeated Bush's father, has departed the scene in a cloud of controversy and is off on a lucrative lecture tour. George Bush Jnr (described, incidentally, in his official cv as an... er... Conservative) is getting on with the business of being president.

Actually I have a theory about that. It goes like this: Hilary Clinton, wife of Bill and who has now entered politics in her own right as a Democrat senator in New York, will stand – and win – the vote for President at the next election, wreaking revenge, in one fell swoop, for George W. Bush's hollow victory and making history at the same time, as the first woman key holder of the White House.

The photographs should make a fine display at the Smithsonian.

Footnote:

After angling myself, without success, for the post of visiting lecturer to the School of Journalism at Columbia with Joan Konnor, the former dean, and then Tom Goldstein, her successor, the news that Al Gore has got the job makes me feel, well, not so bad, I guess.

© Richard Meredith & Mercury Books – all rights reserved

SMALL REVOLUTION STRIKES THE KEYS

Marathon, Florida; January 26

IF IT WASN'T for where it is, I don't suppose anyone would remember Marathon for long.

It strings along US Highway 1; a cluster of homes and businesses built on a coral island in the Florida Keys. In fact, most people would say it's more of a 50-yard dash than anything long distance. You can drive right through it in about four minutes, including a wait at the stop lights.

What kept me there was a sign stuck on a pole near the garage. It said that Marathon had declared itself independent.

There had been a revolution of sorts. The people had spoken. Never mind all the muscle of America in the 21st century, this was personal. Marathon had decided to look after its own destiny, thank you very much. I thought I'd better find out why.

I was actually on my way to Key West, the island at the very end of the Keys, to see where Ernest Hemingway once lived. (– also see *And Finally, it's Papa's Place* in *PASSING THOUGHTS...*) But Wars of Independence don't come along too often in the US of A.

Now before I go on, I ought to tell you some more about this place. The Florida Keys are unique in the American experience - not just for the quality of their ecology, fish and marine life, but also for what the army generals would say was their strategic importance.

Conversely, there would be a devilish problem if they got

Revolution time in Marathon

ONE WAY or ANOTHER

invaded or were struck by a disaster.

Imagine if you will, one side of a necklace of coral dangling for 100 miles or so down from the southern-most State of America and out into the ocean.

Here and there, like knuckles on the chain, islands have built up over thousands of years as sand and silt have solidified on the coral.

Man, in his unceasing ambition, has strung them all together. First with a railway, and then with a road, US 1, connecting them up with bridges and enabling a population of around 80,000 people to build their homes and businesses. On one side of the archipelago lap the blue-green waters of the Gulf of Mexico; on the other, the sterner rollers of the Atlantic. Often, they are only yards apart.

And there they perch, the island Keys, at a precarious average of just four or five feet above the sea. To be honest, if I lived there, I'd get worried if it rained. But there's a whole bunch of bigger problems to consider. Like being in the middle of a Hurricane Alley for one.

America's powers-that-be seem to have mixed feelings about the Keys. The nervous ones see them as an Achilles heel where an enemy could invade (Cuba, for example, is only 90 miles away) and they worry, too, about the logistics of a mass evacuation along just one small highway in the event of a catastrophe – natural or otherwise.

They may be right. It has all the makings of a disaster waiting to happen. Apart from hurricanes, there are threats of tornadoes, waterspouts, oil spills, ship groundings and large fires to think about. Oh, and the outside possibility of a meltdown at Florida Light and Power's nuclear plant at Turkey Point.

A little comfortingly, Florida has designated the Keys an official "Area of Critical Concern" with a hotline system to the Federal Emergency Management Agency, wherever that might be.

On the upside, attracted by some of the world's finest game fishing, wildlife enclaves, coral diving, pleasure boating and beach scenery, it has become one of the nation's top playgrounds. America's riviera.

There is such a surfeit of attractions that three million tourists and holiday-makers turn up every year, multiplying the resident population (and the strain on drainage) 40-fold. Presidents come

SMALL REVOLUTION STRIKES THE KEYS

to spend vacations. Property values have sky-rocketed.

In short, it's an important, dangerously exotic and much-talked-about place. The kind where people start to get excited if there's a spot of revolution going on.

Which brings us back, rather conveniently, to Marathon.

Now, in the normal way of things, there wouldn't be much to get excited about in this 50-yards dash of a place. True, it is one of the larger knuckles on the necklace. But at the last count barely 12,000 folk lived down here.

It's got some romantically-named resort hotel/motels like the Buccaneer and the Banana Bay, a clutch of shops and supermarkets, a neat little library, a surprisingly large Salvation Army hall and – probably quite unconnected – a couple of those outfits where you can hire Adult Videos to keep yourself amused on a quiet night in. I imagine they are rather busy.

There is also a branch office of the local newspaper, an assortment of boat chandlers and fishing tackle places, a set-up where the sheriff shares sub-office facilities with the tax inspector, and a small airstrip with a display of planes on show today which you can usually find replicated in balsawood at Toys 'R' Us.

More substantially, it is bounded at one end by an impressive bridge, seven miles long, which connects it to the next island, and which took such an age to build that workmen nicknamed the place 'marathon' after their epic. It stuck.

*Marathon's harbour:
Home to its floating population in summer*

ONE WAY or ANOTHER

**City Hall:
End of parking lot**

Less substantially, at the other end, is the new city manager's office (to which we shall return) tucked behind a supermarket parking lot.

There is also, I discover, a small harbour out the backside of town which is home for the floating population who visit in high season and which is guarded by a drawbridge. We'll hear more about that later, too.

It is not, I conclude, the world's most obvious hotbed of rebellion. But then again, Marathon's argument will never be bloody. Its struggle is with county hall and its battle of independence is with the authorities. I'll tell you why.

For a long time now, they have been a bolshie lot down on the Keys. And Monroe County, whose job it is to administer the area, has come in for a good hammering.

I suppose the truth of it is that if you are having to cope with an annual invasion of tourists who clog up your one main road, your beaches and your drains AND if you consider that your house might be blown or washed away at any minute by a hurricane, then it's only natural to want your share of any spoils going.

The way Marathon saw it, Monroe County wasn't spending enough of its budget on them and – worse still – they felt it was favouring Key West, Hemingway's affluent island dangling on the end.

After years of wrangling there was nothing else for it. A vote for independence (or incorporation, to use the fancy term). It was all quite constitutional. They went to see an expert, met the criteria, asked the people – and won. Now they've declared their little town a city, elected a council and a mayor, demanded back their share of dues and taxes, and expect to take care of things themselves from here on in.

SMALL REVOLUTION STRIKES THE KEYS

If only pigs could fly. Did you ever hear of something simple happening in politics?

There had to be some horse-trading. Who would be responsible for what? Roads, bridges, street-lighting, emergency services, parks, playgrounds, planning, that disaster scenario... who's going to do it... who's going to pay?

The two sides sat down. The money would have to be split, assets divided, jobs would be lost – and then recreated – new efficiencies, new procedures. It all took some doing. And, of course, some of it didn't get done.

Drawbridge: Huddles in the gate-keeper's hut

Remember the drawbridge? On handover day, they still hadn't decided who should pay the keeper for lifting it up and down to let the big boats in.

"Right then," said the County, "if you're not going to take it over, we'll leave it where it is." And there it stayed, stuck in the upright position, a vertical salute of defiance, while officials from all sides held huddles in the bridge-keeper's hut and worked out

ONE WAY or ANOTHER

a compromise. "Let's be polite and just say there's some confusion over all of this," said Larry, harassed assistant (and soon-to-be editor) of the local newspaper when I called to see him. He said he could go on. And he did. On and on.

"There's a bill in right now for bridge repairs which they are arguing about. Then there's the sewerage issue, and the road widening issue, and the housing issue, and the pollution issue, and they want to trade the cost of garbage collection for the..." My head is beginning to spin. Thankfully a deadline is looming. "Sorry. Got to go. Front page leaves in five minutes," says Larry, beetling off.

"Er, no problem, I think I get the picture," I mutter.

"Why don't you try the new mayor's office," inquired the receptionist thoughtfully, as I went to leave. "Thanks. Good idea," I said.

It took a while. Marathon's City Hall is sliced, like the filling in a weight-watchers sandwich, between a hairdressers and an estate agent at the far end of a parking lot on the outskirts of town.

I'm actually not sure I could have found it at all without the flags outside and a sign in the window.

Inside, I meet Ann, who is somebody in the planning department.

"Oh, there's such a lot to do," she says. "I don't think any of us realized..."

"You're not getting discouraged by independence already are you," I asked, probably too pointedly.

"Oh no, we feel we are really looking after ourselves now; not being just a little part of something so much bigger. You know?"

I said I knew.

"Of course things will be alright when we can get a master plan together. Then we can really work towards something that will make us all feel proud. It's just that there's such a lot to do..."

"M'm," I said, just like before. "I think I get the picture." And I left her to it.

The next conversation is with Ed, who owns the place where I am staying tonight. "Hey, you don't know the half of it," he says. "We are all as mad as prairie dogs down here. Beats me how we all survive. I think it must be the hurricanes that do it. We've had three of the worst ones in America this century, you know?"

SMALL REVOLUTION STRIKES THE KEYS

*Impressive seven-mile bridge with the
old railway alongside*

I said I didn't (*although I did, as it happens; just like I knew that Hurricanes Andrew, Mitch, Georges and, most recently, Debby, have all come calling in the last 10 years and left a big trail of damage*) but Ed was going to tell me anyway.

"Worst of the lot was in '35 – winds of 200 miles an hour and a 20 foot wave that washed away large chunks of the Keys. (*I knew that ,too. Category 5 on the Saffir-Simpson Scale. 800 people died – half of them down this way*).

"It knocked a train clean off the tracks at Islamorada and that put paid to the railways," said Ed.

"Damn things keep buzzin' around all the time. It's no wonder we want to look out for ourselves.

"D'ya know what they want us to do? Evacuate the whole place and all trek off to a school hall in Miami. Can you imagine? Hundreds of thousands of people trying to get up that one small highway and leave everything behind? Are you surprised nobody has any time for the authorities round here?"

Why do I get the feeling that Ed, who owns several motel-type lodging houses on the Keys, is now aboard his favourite hobby-horse?

ONE WAY or ANOTHER

"Yeah, Marathon wants to look after itself. But there'll be plenty of others, you'll see. Big Pine and some of the smaller Keys are waiting to find what happens. Then there's Islamadora, they are going it alone already. It's everyone for himself. We must be a real problem for Monroe – and for the whole State of Florida I guess – but they've only got themselves to blame."

What Ed didn't say (but which I can now share with those of you who don't already know) is that the present rush of independence isn't the biggest show of rebellion on the Keys in recent times.

Twenty years ago on Key West, where the big money is, residents reacted in horror when police blocked off US 1 at the top end for a stop-and-search operation to catch drug runners and illegal immigrants.

Fearing their holiday trade would take fright, the Key Westers quickly went into action.

They fired an old cannon into the ocean, declared themselves a republic, announced they were at war with America, immediately surrendered and then demanded $2billion in foreign aid. The roadblock was removed soon afterwards.

Told you they were a bolshie lot down on the Keys. Like Marathon, I reckon their saga has a long way to run.

Further reading:

Monroe County Comprehensive Emergency Management Plan 1998.
Marathon Incorporation: Budget Impacts 2001, by Monroe County's office of management and budgets.
Monroe County: Sanitary Wastewater Master Plan, June 2000.
Monroe County: Year 2010 Comprehensive Plan.

© Richard Meredith & Mercury Books – all rights reserved

BUMS, ALIENS AND THE URBAN POOR

California; December

JUAN Cesar Gonzales is a Mexican by birth and ambitious by nature. John Francis O'Keefe is half-Irish and half-decent when it comes to computers. Benjamin (Babe) Jackson is black, American, and feels pretty aggravated with the world.

Right now, all of them are living rough on the streets of California.

Of the three, John (Jo Jo) O'Keefe is probably the unluckiest. He's in his early 20's. He's always had a head for figures and a brain which works things through in a logical sequence. He worked in South Park, San Francisco for *MakeitSnappy.com*, producers of the world's first all-in-one digitalized photo album (company slogan: "You snap 'em, we zap 'em"). It was exciting. The job was to analyse customer dems (that's demographics to you and me). It would help with marketing.

The people around him were young and lively. They all expected to make money. Lots of money. And they expected to make it soon. But Jo Jo knew well before most of the others what the sales figures were, so he wasn't surprised when the news came that his job was finished.

It was doubly unfortunate for him that his best friend's girl then decided to move in. The tiny apartment wasn't big enough for all of them. It meant he had to go somewhere else, but there was nowhere else to go. And even the late-night clubs kick you out at 3 or 4 am.

Juan's story is rather different. With his swarthy good looks and teasing smile, he fancied himself as a big movie star or, let's be honest, maybe something smaller then, like a regular on one of those TV soaps.

From his boyhood town of La Paz on Mexico's Pacific Peninsula he tried everything he could to get himself a break. Pictures, specially posed (and expensive) to the agencies, letters by the score, phone calls to everyone he'd ever known who might get him that first introduction. After all, he had the looks, the

ONE WAY or ANOTHER

Homeless and hungry in United Nations Plaza out front of city hall

husky voice. The women loved him, didn't they?

Time passed. Juan got desperate. So what if they had enough homegrown heart-throbs already? If only someone up there in Los Angeles could see him. Just once...

It was scary getting past the border guards in the desert that night. And God, didn't his treacherous fellow countrymen rip him off for all those new identity papers? And then what? Worked in a kitchen in the Gaslamp Quarter of San Diego for next to nothing until the boss got fed up with his moaning and threw him out. But who could he tell?

Benji (well no man wants to be called Babe do they?) is 42 going on 60. He lives, if that's the right word, around Market and Mission streets in San Francisco although, let's face it, he moves about quite a bit. Tonight he'll go up a couple of blocks to Union Square. There's some fancy hotels there, which is good because they throw out better quality garbage and it's always warmer round the back of their kitchens.

It must be 20 years since he arrived in the city, using up virtually

BUMS, ALIENS AND THE URBAN POOR

every last cent on the journey by bus and train across from li'l ol' Moss Bluff, Louisiana. Still, what kind of life could he make for himself there?

Round here in the Tenderloin area, everybody knows him. He's cagey about the gangs who think it's sport to give him a good kicking, and he's been arrested for vagrancy more times than he's been boozed out of his mind (which is really saying something). Sometimes he forgets what day of the week it is. But then again, that doesn't seem to matter much.

I got to meet Juan, Jo Jo and Benji (not their real names) on the streets of California. For one reason or another luck has run out on them. Now they are bums. Or beggars. Or hobos. Or aliens. Or drifters. The underclass. The urban poor. And there are thousands more like them; which is daft really, because this is one of the most wealthy places on earth.

More people live in California than any other State in the USA. There were 3.4 million of them last time they counted although, quite probably, that didn't include Juan, Jo Jo or Benji and all the others with no fixed abodes. How could it? After all, that's just what it means, they don't live anywhere.

It has the second largest city in the whole of North America (Los Angeles) and arguably its most cosmopolitan (San Francisco), a climate which is legendarily good, soil which is, for the most part, productively fertile, and a coastline fit for dreamin'.

Not surprisingly, the allure is all-consuming. In London, they used to say the streets were paved with gold. In California, in many places, you can quite expect to see walls papered with $100 bills. Over the last 10 years, its population has grown by more than any other State's, and it's not hard to see why. Trouble is, for all those who've made it, an awful lot haven't.

In West Hollywood, that most affluent area of Los Angeles, where film stars shop in Sunset Boulevard and pet poodles with diamond collars go for walkies round the leafy lanes of Bel Air, life is a gotto, according to an article I read the other day. Not a ghetto, you understand, but a gotto.

"What's a gotto," the inventor, a woman by the it-can-only-be-American name of Faith Popcorn, was asked.

"It's a place where folks have gotto lotto bucko," said Ms Popcorn, who has apparently made herself a fortune by crystal

ONE WAY or ANOTHER

ball-gazing future products for big corporations.

Have no doubt about it, the creed in California is every man for himself. But for those who haven't gotto lotto, and where home is still spelled ghetto, soft or hard landings have far more to do with a choice of bed for the night than the nation's economy.

In parts of Inglewood where I stayed on south central Los Angeles, you don't walk on the street, you don't go out after dark, and you don't go to some places at all if your skin is the wrong colour.

For Juan, and the thousands like him who come up from Mexico, many never reach Los Angeles, although it's less than 150 miles across the border. You find them – unless the police get to them first – on the streets of border towns like San Diego.

No wonder so many Mexicans are willing to risk everything to get into California. The contrast is blindingly stark: California, with all its wealth and opportunity; Mexico, where 4 out of every 10 families live in what is described as "extreme poverty" and 1 in 10 people cannot read or write.

According to some statistics I've read, virtually 40% of Mexicans live on 26 pesos ($3) or less, each day. And that's for everything. I reckon the average Californian spends about the same on brushing his teeth in the morning. By comparison, their income is more than $70 a day.

Poor Mexico. To think that they ruled most of the lands which became the State, if you see what I mean, little more than 150 years ago. Not only that, but within a year of signing away the place under the Treaty of Guadalupe Hidalgo in 1848, John Sutter's mob discovered the gold – and we all know what happened after that. The Mexicans must have felt gutted.

Despite its size, mainland America only has two borders. The Canadian one up north stretches for 4,000 miles and is, by all accounts, the longest unguarded border in the world. The line with Mexico lasts for only half that distance, but it keeps a small army of State troopers extremely busy. Speaks for itself don't you think?

They call them illegal aliens down in southern California – the rag, tag and bobtailers who try to slip unnoticed across the 25 miles of no-man's-land which marks the long line from Tijuana in the west to Matamoros in the east.

There's 100 million Mexicans, and although they don't all

BUMS, ALIENS AND THE URBAN POOR

Parking lot for the residentially challenged in San Francisco

want to get into America, you won't be surprised to hear that many thousands finish up like Juan, exploited as cheap labour by profiteering bosses (despite the threat of big fines), and looking over their shoulder every day in fear they get discovered.

My uncle, who lives not far from the border in Phoenix, Arizona, reckons there are 6,000 people living rough even in that well-sanitized city. And many of them will be Mexican aliens.

It's a dangerous game, running the gauntlet across the border. Much of the terrain is inhospitable and there are several large ranges used by US forces for live gunnery and bombing practice. "Border deaths" are officially running at one a day.

Mexico's new President, Vicente Fox (yes, really), a one-time Coca-Cola truck driver (also really), is apparently so embarrassed by the tidal wave of his citizens disappearing over the horizon that he has appointed a minister with special responsibility for tightening up border security. Mind you, since Mr Ernesto Ruffo is said to own businesses on both sides of the barbed-wire, so to speak, it

ONE WAY or ANOTHER

**Drum-rolls
for the passers-by help with street collection**

will be interesting to see where he positions himself.

Meanwhile, up in San Francisco, life on the streets with Jo Jo and Benji is a lot more visible – and, dare I say it, risable. Appropriately, in this city of innovation, it is also a lot more enterprising.

Which is how I can tell you of a new initiative among the residentially challenged of San Francisco. They have become horizontally mobile. I had better explain.

They have discovered the mobile home, although you and I would know it better as the humble supermarket trolley. You see them everywhere. And, since this is the place where history shows that trends begin, I guess I can confidently predict that I've seen the new universal transport system for the underfunded.

Packed inside is the typical hobo's survival kit – blanket, change of clothes (optional), black plastic bin liner, usually containing an assortment of cans and bottles carefully selected from the city's garbage bins for their recycle cashback value, spare shoes (preferable), hopefully dangling from the basket's grill-

BUMS, ALIENS AND THE URBAN POOR

work to give them air, and a hoard of cardboard and newspapers which make for a handy mattress when it's time to kip down somewhere for the night.

The cops in this tolerant city, which has a name for the unexpected, are more inclined to move the bums about than arrest them. Which presents an unusual sight when you spot a sequence of them, rolling along like a wagon train, after the police have moved on a road-full. Can you picture the scene? Well, imagine a conga between Tesco's or Walmart and the Salvation Army hostel on a busy Friday night.

They congregate, too, often under the shelter of bridges and awnings, to form what might be called a mobile home park in the street theatre of the absurd.

It's only people like me, I suppose, doing a grand tour of the towns and cities of California, who can make an assessment about the extent of homelessness in this most affluent State. Well, me and all those people who are meant to know about these things officially, of course.

You can make some handy comparisons. For instance, I can tell you that the needy who try to give entertainment value, even if it isn't much good, will stand a far better chance of persuading passers-by to part with their cash.

The best example I ever saw was a group of five drop-outs in Sydney, Australia, each wearing shirts of different bright colours, who walked

Christmas on the sidewalk

up and down the street in a row, always in unison – now stopping, now starting, now crossing the street, now recrossing it. Their act was so effective, it even brought the traffic to a halt. And they collected a small fortune.

In California, I saw no such troupe, but in this month before Christmas I was treated to several attempts at festive carols

ONE WAY or ANOTHER

including a funky version of "Rudolph the red-nosed reindeer" played by a man who accompanied himself with drum-rolls on a set of upturned plastic containers and an old-style hotel ashtray.

There was also, rather painfully, a rendition of "'Tis the Season to be Jolly ..." sung by an Irish-American who took swigs between verses from a bottle in brown paper which would have put zest into the fuel tank of a jumbo.

I am able to report, too, on a new trade developing down in the gutter. It's called sign-writing. What you do, is sit on the pavement looking as dishevelled as possible, and hold up a piece of cardboard on which you have composed the most emotive message imaginable.

Charity has become a very competitive business. Pleas like "Homeless", "Hungry" and Help me" are taken as merely standard. So are various specifics like: Money needed for such-and-such an operation, cash to feed abandoned pets, and support required for any number of children or disadvantaged relatives.

But my favourites, such is my perverse and imbalanced sense of humour, are the witty ones.

"Long hair and a surfboard to support"
– seen at Venice Beach, Los Angeles.

"Big bash, need cash"
– alleged road accident victim in San Diego.

"Homeless? My ass! I just want to get high"
– San Francisco.

© Richard Meredith & Mercury Books – all rights reserved

SHAKEN BY AN ECONOMIC EARTHQUAKE

San Francisco, California; December 12

I HAVE never been in an earthquake before. But it feels like I'm in one now. I swear the ground is shaking and the sky has turned a darker shade of grey. I am standing in Montgomery Street, San Francisco. I shouldn't be surprised; they get a lot of earthquakes round here.

In America, Montgomery Street is known as the Wall Street of the West. It runs through the heart of San Francisco's financial district. A couple of blocks from where I am standing it is crossed by Sutter Street, named after John Sutter, the local hero who started the Gold rush which set California on its way to becoming one of the wealthiest places on earth.

There will be more of that later. But, for the moment, let's just say that this is one of the more important places to feel an earthquake coming on. And I'm in the middle of it.

Well OK, to be precise, I'm in the *virtual reality* of it. In actual fact, the road is shaking because two large security vans, built like armoured trucks, are juddering past me in a rush, picking up the takings from several local companies. As it happens, their loads are a fair bit lighter than usual.

It also occurs to me that the sky is dark because in the financial center of this extraordinary city, many of the buildings are so tall they simply cut out the light.

Nevertheless, I'm still pretty sure there's an earthquake going on.

Sitting on the sidewalk, with a paper cup in his outstretched hand, is a beggar cadging quarters from passers-by. Up above him, on one of those natty moving neon signs, is a flicker-tape message which says the Nasdaq is down by another 80 points. It makes for a poignant cameo of what's happening.

Fact is, Californians are used to disasters. In less than 100 years they have had more than their fair share. There have been three earthquakes which killed people. Altogether, a whole lot of people. And another one could happen any minute.

ONE WAY or ANOTHER

Ups and downs of life in Montgomery Street

On the other hand, there have been more than enough good times to compensate: The Goldrush of 150 years ago which put them on the map, the megabucks movie business down the road in Los Angeles, and the New Technology industry which has grown up right around here most recently.

Throw in a few invasions – like the Beatniks of the 1950s, the Hippies of the 1960s, and the Gays of whenever since – and you would definitely be forgiven for thinking that this place has been hurtling through the greatest switchback ride in history.

Come to think of it, there must be a good few Californians alive today who have been through all of it except the Goldrush. All of it by God; every up and down of it, every twist-and-turn of it. No wonder they want to get rich quick in these parts. Because tomorrow ...

But I digress.

Recession is a word which economists might liken to the tremors before an earthquake. Unrestrained, it can lead to a Great Depression, which is the super biggie; the kind that has ruined businessmen reaching for a pistol in the filing cabinet, or rushing to join the Society of Bungee jumping for the Unattached.

Things aren't that way yet. But today, in San Francisco, I'd take a sizeable bet that I am at the epicenter of, shall we say, a significant realignment of the financial landscape – although, truth to tell, only history will show if this was precisely the time and exactly the place where it all began.

What's happening is that the dotcom sector of the New Technology revolution is going bust. Put in simple terms – of which the Americans have a happy knack – it's a "tech-wreck"; a burn out. And California is the local crematorium. I'll tell you why ...

Roughly 30 years ago, when Mr J. C. R. Licklider (yes, really) and his team of boffins funded by the US defence department,

SHAKEN BY AN ECONOMIC EARTHQUAKE

first thought up the idea of an electronic internet, they opened a pandora's box which would revolutionise our ability to communicate with one another.

We all know what has happened since. In theory, if not in fact, computer science has brought us the opportunity to improve the speed and efficiency of virtually every task and occupation known to Man. It has also, mind-bogglingly, overwhelmed us with a plethora of equipment, gadgets and gizmos which you have to be a teenager, or younger, to understand.

Anyhow, we are meant to keep everyone informed about what is going on through the internet; the worldwide web. It's a very simple and clever concept, and it's just the kind of thing which people make a fortune out of in California. Or did do. Or still hope to, if you get my drift.

This is the place, they say, where enterprise is an act of faith and optimism is a religion. It is also, not surprisingly, where you can find most of the action when there's a technical revolution going on.

Which brings us round, after a fashion, to the dotcom contingent – or, rather, to the earthquake which is destroying them – and to the reason why I think I'm in on the death.

Not that California has the monopoly on dotty-coms, of course. Or even dotty-ness. But I am told that you can find more of them/it in Silicon Valley than anywhere else.

Should I explain Silicon Valley? Well, it's a rather mystical stretch of office and factory hi-tech utopia which, for want of a better description, lies between Highways 101 and Interstate 5 which run in parallel down the west coast from Seattle to Los Angeles via San Francisco.

I am tempted to point out that Microsoft, the biggest name in computers, is at one end of it, and that Warner Brothers, probably the

Sign of the times: Nasdaq index hits an all-time low (– also see Nasdaq is Virtual Reality in PASSING THOUGHTS...)

ONE WAY or ANOTHER

biggest name in disaster movies, is at the other. But perhaps I'm hinting at a connection that really isn't there.

Meanwhile, back at the dotty-coms, no one seems able to find out exactly who came up with the naively flawed idea that all you need to make an e-fortune is to take a service or product, pop a hype-load of information about it onto the web, and then sell it in huge quantities to people all around the world.

If they did, I'm not even sure the electric chair would be good enough.

Oh that making money was so easy! In fact, I suppose, it was the very simplicity of the idea which provided its fatal attraction. Enterprise is a religion round here, remember? So the investors – otherwise known as speculators – said their prayers every night and threw billions at it.

Trouble is, as the world and his wife now knows, it takes more than billions to persuade enough folk to buy the whatever-it-is from a dotty-com site – even if they can find it to begin with. Couple that with an almost evangelical need by many of the proprietors to work in fancy-Dan offices, to pay themselves fancy-Dan salaries, and to live out fancy-Dan lifestyles, and what have you got? Answer: earthquake economics of seismic proportions.

I am in California just before Christmas. The reality is, only history will tell if this was the time and this was the place. But right now it certainly feels like the Financial Earth is moving big-time.

As is the way of these things, there have been some prior warnings. Just nine months ago, the Nasdaq index, which is America's daily measure of the worth of hi-tech companies, was at an all-time high. Today it is at an all-time low.

In between, the sound of crashing dotcom companies has been echoing all around. Many of them have been here in San Francisco, and many of them have had names sounding about as daft as their business plans. Here's just a few: *DrKoop.com*, *Send.com*, *Boo.com* and *MotherNature.com*.

Today there is news of another fatality – *Kibu.com*, a company whose idea it was to capture the hearts, minds and pocket-money of teenage girls with the aim of selling them appropriate products by the handbagfull. They call it on-line focused marketing.

Anyway, you can guess what happened. The proprietors set up in fancy-Dan offices, paid themselves fancy-Dan salaries etc etc, and then, in practically no time at all, they got through a shed-

SHAKEN BY AN ECONOMIC EARTHQUAKE

load – no, it was actually more like a container load – of OPM (that's Other People's Money), promoting and advertising a site that (a) hardly anyone visited, and consequently, (b) no one bought anything from.

At least the bosses appear to have waved the white flag before the cupboard was completely bare.

Just another burned-out wreck among the pile of dotty-com ashes? Maybe. But now I'm not certain. After all, there always has to be one last straw; a time when enough is enough; a place where the writing is on the wall; a day when the wheels come off; a moment when the earthquake strikes.

I find that the Nasdaq has dropped with another hefty thud. I see a headline in the paper which says, in effect, that the dotcom game is over. Maybe this is it then: On this day in this month of December 2000, and in this place called California?

And yet, I hear you ask, so what if a few billion – no, make that a few trillion – dollars of Other People's Money have gone down the tubes? So what (if I have heard it correctly) that around 20, 000 people have lost their jobs round here in the last month alone? So what. It's hardly enough to shake the world, surely?

Ah yes, but here's the rub – for let's not forget where we are. This isn't called the Golden State for nothing. If it was a country, the economy, as measured by Gross Domestic Product (GDP), would be the sixth largest in the world. In the league table of these things, only the rest of North America, Japan and Germany, come significantly higher. It's bigger than China and virtually on a par with France and the UK.

Get the picture? Size does matter. This is the place where they measure things on the Richer – as well as the Richter – Scale. When they get the financial jitters in California, an awful lot of people catch the bug.

The proof is in the indices of Stock Markets all across the world. I check the paper. Tech stock prices are falling everywhere. What's happening to the New Age Economy in California is psychologically shattering. Confidence is plummeting. Those economic earthquake shockwaves are spreading. So hold on tight for the next, exciting rollercoaster ride!

Which kind of brings us back to John Sutton and how it all began, and why no one in California should be surprised by whatever type of earthquake strikes them next.

ONE WAY or ANOTHER

Scene of the 'Greatest switchback ride in history'

Safety sign: Earthquake engineers do their work

The first gold-bearing ore was discovered on land owned by Capt Sutton down in the western foothills of the Sierra Nevadas. Apparently he told a newspaper editor friend but swore him to secrecy. Mad fool! A few front page headlines later and sleepy San Francisco, then just a huddle of 200 homes and 800 people, was truly on the map.

The Goldrush of 1849 was under way, bringing 60,000 fortune hunting hopefuls trekking in from across the nation, or sailing in from overseas, and transforming the place into a cosmopolitan city almost overnight.

Boomtime No.2 has been altogether different. It began in 1908 with the birth of an entertainments industry which grew big through flickering, voiceless camera images, rolled on into movies, TV and recording, spawned Hollywood and Disneyland along the way, and developed the celluloid city of Los Angeles

SHAKEN BY AN ECONOMIC EARTHQUAKE

into the world's greatest star-making (and sometimes breaking) machine.

Then, dating from the 1960s, came Boomtime No.3 with the dawning of the Information Era or the New Economy or the Whatever-else-you-want-to-call-it-as-long-as-it's-not-the Dotcom Era, much stirrings in Silicon Valley, and the birth of a multi-billion-dollar, hi-tech industry.

Most places are lucky if they benefit from one Boomtime. Californians have had three. Plus, it must be said, more than their fair share of baby-boomers – like silver, oil and government defence contracts.

But in this land which would surely scoop every prize for topsy turvyness, they have also witnessed some appalling earthquakes.

If, like me, you struggle to remember what teacher described as a cwm or a corrie, or even a circue, in the geography class, then you will only have the vaguest notion about what causes earthquakes. Just for you, however, I looked it up in a book. They say it is caused by the movement of tectonic plates just under the earth's surface. San Francisco apparently straddles the Eastern Pacific and North American plates and when they move, whatever happens is usually the fault of San Andreas.

All I can say is that he's been very busy. After what I read to have been a "sizeable earthquake" in 1868, the Big One came in 1906, decimating most of San Francisco, killing 3,000 people and leaving over 100,000 homeless.

In 1989 came another, causing extensive damage and 67 deaths; and then another, in 1994, down towards Los Angeles, which killed 72 and ruined the homes of 22,000.

Amazing, eh? And sobering, too. Being practical people, and no doubt fatalistic (well, wouldn't you be if your hometown was being hit by an earthquake more often than you know what's good for you?) I find that tradesfolk are not at all averse to advertising goods and services to help in a holocaust.

I note with interest, too, that all new construction must have flexibility and safety features built in, especially for high buildings. So that's good to know then!

There is even a section devoted to an earthquake "first aid and survival guide" in the local telephone book. One rule reads: "(if you are) in a crowded public place, do NOT rush for the exits. Stay calm and encourage others to do the same."

Perhaps they should put a sign up like that in Montgomery Street.

I think of it again today as I listen to the virtually real sounds of plunging stock prices, crashing profit forecasts and exploding (or should that be imploding?) Balance Sheets.

On TV I am told that elsewhere in America the Big Three carmakers are all cutting back on production; a leading steel-maker is about to go bust; and one of the oldest names in retail is closing 250 stores. The country's main stock index, the Dow Jones, is at its lowest level for 20 years, national growth is slowing fast; profit-making is at a standstill...

Maybe you will say I am carrying the earthquake analogy too far. But I am not so sure.

There's a whole lot of shaking going on. And, here in California, the symbolism of an earthquake striking the economy seems inescapable.

Footnotes:

Jan 3: The Fed, in an emergency move to boost the economy, cuts interest rates by 0.5%.

January: Nat Assoc of Purchasing Managers says US manufacturing already in recession.

Jan 17: Emergency funding approved in California to avoid power utilities going broke.

Jan 27: World Economic Forum asks: Is US slowdown dragging world into recession?

Jan 31: Fed cuts interest rates another 0.5%. (This month's total 1% is the most for a decade).

February: Last month's jobs loss total is highest since recording began.

Feb 8: President Bush announces $1.6trillion tax cuts plan to boost economy and confidence.

March 14: Japanese admit 19 largest banks are on verge of collapse.

March 16: Dow suffers worst one-week points drop in 11 years.

March 20: Fed cuts interest rates another 0.5%.

April: Dow's points loss in Quarter 1 is 8.4% – most for 23 years.

© Richard Meredith and Mercury Books – all rights reserved

NAME-DROPPING WITH THE GREATEST

Los Angeles; November 22

HE SITS at the front of the bus. Tall, slim, mid-20's. Reminds me of a young *Tom Hanks*. Above the sassy smile and mandatory shades, his tawny hair pulls back off the forehead and flops down in classic *Hugh Grant* style.

This is Gary, professional name-dropper. A master of the moniker. "Hi guys," he says. "Welcome to Los Angeles."

It's 10am. There are about 1,000 buses just like ours setting off around this city about now. They are full with folk of every age and every nation. Many of ours are ladies who won't see 40 again. It matters not a jot. Male or female, young or old, Gary will refer to us all as *guys* throughout the trip. That's the way it is in La La land.

Everyone likes to hear about the rich and famous; to see where they live, they shop, they eat. Somehow it's like you're sharing part of their lives; of being famous, too. Gary is making us feel like that. It's how he earns a living. And he's very good at it.

For those of us who've already checked the map, it's clear we are in for quite a day.

Along the coast – Fisherman's Village, Little Venice, Santa Monica; along the streets – Wilshire Boulevard, Sunset Strip, Rodeo Drive; through the suburbs – Beverly Hills, Bel Air, Hollywood ...

We are out for a bit of celeb spotting. That's what Gary's job is all about. There's a target list of thousands. To listen to him, you'd think he knows them all. But then, maybe we all think we do.

We start at Marina del Rey with the fishermen. It's said to be the biggest man-made marina in the world. There are around 10,000 yachty playthings of the super-rich slapping idly on their moorings.

Mind you, they say that a lot round here. You know, the biggest marina, the greatest this, the largest that. It's not at all out of place to talk in the most unique superlatives. "See that over there?

ONE WAY or ANOTHER

Working out on Venice Beach attracts the crowds

It's the world's biggest solar-powered ferris wheel," says Gary.

Oh yeah, and who are you kidding? I think to myself. (I check it out later. Guess what? Headline in next issue of *Variety* magazine reads: Writer eats world's largest slice of humble pie.)

Anyway, sadly, like we all know, everything cannot be super-biggy-besty-whatsit all the time. "So, if I tell you that this is the place where one of the *Beachboys* sailed to his death, and that *Natalie Wood*, wife of the actor *Robert Wagner*, drowned, you can see that these kind of people are only like the rest of us," advises Gary solemnly. M'm, I think I know what he means, although I can't say I'm absolutely sure.

Not an especially joyfull opening scene, right enough. But there's better news on the way to Venice Beach. Why, here's the school where that flaxen-haired swooner *Robert Redford* spent his early years, according to Gary. Oh, and here's the courthouse where civil lawyers for football star *O. J. Simpson* (accused of killing his beautiful wife and her handsome young waiter friend) argued long and hard to clear his name.

It's the same courthouse, apparently, where *Elvis Presley* tied the knot with *Priscilla*. We all peer at the neat stone building almost expecting the couple to come bounding down the steps. I am wondering if they sell jailhouse rock in the souvenir shop.

NAME-DROPPING WITH THE GREATEST

Picture collage of the VIP Hollywood Bus Tour

At Venice Beach, things start hotting up – in every sense. This is the place where the skateboard was invented, intoned Gary. It is also the place, apparently, where the *Baywatch* babes practiced their breast strokes. Was there any connection, I question vaguely. My mind being somewhere else by now, you understand.

"Oh, and *Arnie* (note the familiarity of the first name terms) *Schwarzenegger* (on the other hand, let's be practical, maybe it's just that Arnie is a lot easier to say) used to practice his body-building down there in the open air gym," says Gary. "Now he's got a restaurant here." Where the beefsteak must be rather rare, I am tempted to add.

By complete contrast, we hear, the annual Chocoholics Festival is held just around the corner. Amusing, huh?

In the United States only New York is larger than this amazing, sprawling city of Los Angeles. But there is nowhere in the world with more celebrities to the square mile.

And I mean celebrity – as in somebody a lot better known than us guys on a $77 name-dropping bus jaunt from VIP Tours & Charters Sightseeing Corp. Someone like *Monica Lewinski*, for example, a mere intern at the White House, who grew up just over there, says Gary pointing somewhere in the distance rather less firmly than he had before.

ONE WAY or ANOTHER

I look for Monica, the girl who paid lip-service to her President. Maybe just one glance of that voluptuous figure, that pouting mouth? But no, there's only a rather ample woman on the sidewalk doing the shopping with her three small kids.

We are now, I notice, turning inland into Sunset Boulevard. At about 20 miles long, it is one of the longest streets in the world (those superlatives again), and, more to the point, one of the most famous.

It goes through Beverly Hills, that sell-u-light suburb. It's just 5.5 square miles, but 34,000 residents have made it one of the richest neighbourhoods in the universe. Early film immortals *Mary Pickford* and *Douglas Fairbanks* were part of the scene here, says our chief ND (Name Dropper), while new faces on the block include *Telly Savalas* (aka *Kojak*) and our own *Tom Jones*, the voice from the valleys.

But the guys really get excited when we chug up the hills to Bel Air. For it's here that the hugely biggest reputations hang out and the houses are the stuff of pure fantasy: French style chateaux, mock Georgian mansions, ranchless ranch houses. Or, at least, I think they are. It's hard to tell when you are peering through undergrowth as thick as a jungle from the back of a bus.

We are down to a crawl; being asked to gaze over walls, look around trees, peek through windows with wrought-iron grilles. They like their privacy, smoothes Gary, making light of it.

Privacy? Don't make me laugh! Let's do some numbers: With 1,000 buses a day doing the city tour, let's say half of them come up here to Bel Air. In an eight-hour day, that's 60-odd an hour, or one every minute.

A bus-load of tourists, paid good money to gawp into your life, pulling up outside your gate every minute of the day. And they expect privacy? A goldfish should be so lucky.

"See that roof over there?" says Gary, "that's where *Jack Lemmon* has a place. And this one (the birds on the gateposts give it away) was *Alfred Hitchcock's*."

He promises us that *Clarke Gable* had "that one" (presumably the one with the fancy pointed bits at each end of the roof) and that *Burt Bacharat* (he of the rained-on head) is "somewhere over there." ND points vaguely at a large dark shape hidden behind a bunch of thick trees.

Most of the houses, he confesses, are rented out (which, of

course, hugely reduces our chances of celeb-spotting). So now you tell us! But here, apparently, is a real lived-in residence. It's *Elizabeth Taylor's* pad, we are told. From the comfort of our mobile gallery, we stare at two tightly-shut wooden gates and a sullen-looking wheelie bin. No Dame Elizabeth today then – although we are assured that she is here for most of the time.

No luck either with rock music star *Elton John.* Actually it's too soon for him. He's having a place built here right now, says Gary, drawing our gaze to a monumental pile of bricks, sand and assorted other building materials in a heap beside the road.

Real estate values are stratospheric, we are given to understand (and who would doubt it?). $10 million is a conservative average. One place, belonging to a film producer, if I heard it right, has a see-through swimming pool in his garden. Our bus is below it on the road. We all stare up hopefully expecting to see... well, maybe some famous underbelly doing frogleg kicks I suppose. But oh dear, the pool is empty. "Must be cleaning day today," states Gary.

"Ah, now's here's a good one," encourages our leader. "This one's where *Ron* and *Nancy Reagan* are moving in." A home from home, you might say, for the former President whose path to fame began locally as a bit-part actor in B-rated cowboy movies and later took him into politics as California's State governor.

An interesting story here. "The number of the house was 666," says Gary with a chuckle. "Now that's the Devil's number."

Nancy Regan

...and the old fella...

ONE WAY or ANOTHER

Immortalised in concrete outside Mann's Chinese Theatre

We all giggle. "So they've had it changed to 668." We check the letter-box. 668 is what it says. Shame the Reagans aren't out there collecting their mail. It would have been nice to see the old fella.

"OK guys," exhorts Gary once more, seemingly not the least bit discouraged that we have yet to actually catch sight of a real celebrity. "Let's go and see where these folk do their shopping." The bus eases its way off Sunset and into Rodeo Drive.

Here, the names are like a who's-who of the fashion business. *Hermes, la Coste, Gucci, Bally, Christian Dior, Hilfiger...* I notice a *Burberry's* sign, too, from merrie olde England. How nice. Then I spot a Super Sale notice on their window. Shame about that.

"Mostly you have to shop by appointment round here," says our leader. "In fact, if you promise to spend enough cash, they'll close the store and you can have it all to yourself." Ah, so that's what they mean by personal attention.

Our ND is full of anecdotes. It helps to keep us amused instead of us harping on about all those celebs we have yet to spot. "See this building here," we gape left-hand side at what was apparently once a restaurant famed for its home-made chilli. "The recipe was a secret, but the stars loved it so much they would even send their drivers down to collect a take-away." Hey, that's a good one.

Oh, and over here (we scramble to the other side), right along from the HQ of *Hugh Heffner's* Playboy empire, is the Cedars-Sinai medical centre. Is there a connection? "Know what that is," questions Gary. The guys look suitably blank. "It's where *Frank Sinatra* died. And," he adds quickly before we all shed tears, "it's also the place where *Catherine Zeta-Jones* (wife of actor *Michael*

NAME-DROPPING WITH THE GREATEST

Douglas) has just had her baby." The oohs turn to aahs.

Time for the bus to rumble on. Next stop Hollywood – America's ultimate home of entertainment; and, of course, another lexicon of legends for Gary, our very own guide to the stars.

It's impossible to miss the place. The name is on the hill, high above us, in letters 45ft tall. It must be the biggest signpost in the world. "The idea is that visitors should be able to see it when they come out of the airport 10 miles away," we hear. Cor!

Down on the street, meanwhile, we are invited to step into the feet of greatness. Quite literally. Outside *Mann's* Chinese theatre, for reasons of which I am still not quite sure, there are 150 paving slabs with the names, hands and footprints of many of the biggest stars in showbiz immortalized in concrete.

I look them over. *Sean Connery* and *John Travolta* are among the latest. Many of the earlier ones, I notice, have messages of dedication to Sid.

"Thanks two million Sid," says one.

"For Sid, the world's greatest showman," says another.

Who is Sid? I wonder. Over to Gary. Turns out he was *Sid Grauman*, a big-time impresario in the early days who gave many of the budding stars their chance. Must have made a big impression on them then. Ho ho!

Now here's some marble and bronze star shapes, set into the pavement down either side of Hollywood Boulevard, with the names of cinema greats etched on them. There's more than 2,000 in this 2.5-mile Walk of Fame, according to the guide book. Need help to find your favourite? No problem, the Chamber of Commerce has an identification officer ready and waiting on a toll-free number.

Stars for stars on the Walk of Fame

ONE WAY or ANOTHER

Outside Mann's theatre, competition is hotting up. The man in the official ticket hut is hawking a tour of 50 celebrity homes to a gaggle of camera-clicking Japanese, while from the pavement nearby, an agitated man with a stetson and beard is shouting at them that he'll do it for $15 less. Seems like you can even get a discount on the price of fame.

But now it's time to go; time to visit the next hideout on this day of hunting the most-elusive, lesser-spotted celebrity bird. We are off to *Universal Studios*, says Gary. It is, needless to say, the biggest studio complex in the world. They have made about 8,000 films here since things began around 1908.

He starts to name some. I start to feel queasy.

"Then there's all the other studios around town," says Gary, obviously intent on running down the names like the credits in a blockbuster. "*Warner Brothers, 20th Century Fox, Paramount...*"

I can definitely feel a headache coming on.

"And, of course, there's *Disneyland* which has a kingdom all to itself over there at Anaheim..."

I can spot a commercial on the way. And, sure enough, Gary doesn't disappoint. "Now VIP do a special tour to ..."

But my mind is already switched off. Gone blank. I am done with non-spottable celebrities. I am numb from names. I have peaked on personalities. Flipped out on fame. OD'd on idolatry.

"I'm sorry," I tell Gary as he heads the other guys in the direction of Universal's turnstiles. "I think I'll have to go and lie down for a bit; look, I don't suppose there's a casting couch handy, is there?"

© Richard Meredith & Mercury Books – all rights reserved

PASSING THOUGHTS...PASSING THOUGHTS

A miscellany of the bizarre, the unusual, and even the interesting, from around the world.

VIVE LA DIFFERENCE

With the Channel Tunnel, the euro and the EU, Britain's relationship with the French these days is more *entente cordiale* than *intente mortelle* – but things were very different in Canada three and four centuries ago. *Les francais,* who set up shop on Canada's east coast in 1608, called the place New France and there were fights galore with the rival Brits. Much of the action centred around Quebec city (which both sides valued as an entry port down the St Lawrence to the land and lakes further south) where the French built a fort and called it the capital of their new empire.

Six times the city was under siege and as often as not the British sent in a fleet to reinforce their attacks. The turning point came in 1759 after the Brits famously climbed the cliffs in darkness and stormed the citadel. The opposing armies then fought the Battle of Quebec on land alongside known as the Plains of Abraham. It only lasted 20 minutes – but that was time enough for the English general James Wolfe to be killed and for the French leader Le Marquis de Montcalm to get mortally wounded. It went down as a victory to *les anglais* and the French were never quite the same again; handing over any rights they thought they had to Canada under the Treaty of Paris in 1763.

Mind you, French is still the first language in Quebec province and not long ago the separatist movement all but won a referendum to go their own way from the Crown. The Plains of Abraham is now a 250-acre leisure and pleasure

ONE WAY or ANOTHER

area known simply as Battlefields Park and a magnificent hotel, the medieval looking *Chateau Frontenac* sits on the site of the old fort. Churchill and Roosevelt met there in World War II to plan the D-Day landings... in France.

COLD COMFORT AT THE STORE

It may be darned cold outside, but nothing's going to stop the Canadians from doing their shopping. In Montreal, where winters last six months and brass monkeys regularly lose parts of their anatomy, the population goes underground to get their groceries. In the *Ville Souterraine* there are 30kms of streetwalks, 1,700 shops and 200 restaurants. Alternatively, in Calgary, they go up instead of down with a "+15 Walkway" network of covered-in bridges and passageways round the city center which link main buildings like shopping malls, hotels, government offices, the library and city hall. All the walkways are 15ft (4.6m) above the roads – hence the system's name – which I guess is fine unless you happen to be driving a truck 15ft 6ins tall, or a double-decker bus.

LIQUID ASSETS

Canada, with the Great Lakes and all its wonderful rivers, has the most fresh water in the world – about 25% (the actual proportion naturally varies depending on the weather!). In America, it is estimated that 10% of the people own 85% of the nation's financial, property or corporate wealth.

HOLD ON TO YOUR PENOBSCOT

Fort Knox in Kentucky is the place where America keeps its gold reserves with legendary security. But there's another Fort Knox which not so many people know about. Fort Knox Mark II, a site of historic interest, sits on a cliff on the Atlantic estuary of the Penobscot river in Maine looking across towards Bucksport. In 1779, before it was built and Britain still ruled the local waves, an American fleet of 45 ships plus 2,000 soldiers was given a bloody nose by 750 British troops, three sloops and four transport carriers, when they tried to capture Fort George in nearby Castine.

The Penobscot Expedition, as it was diplomatically called, was America's worst naval disaster prior to Pearl Harbour. Later efforts to dislodge the Brits in the War of 1812 also failed, so when control was finally ceded to them, the Americans vowed never again to lose their Penobscot.

They figured that folk would always be raiding up the river trying to capture Bangor, which was the center of a valuable lumber trade, so they built Fort Knox with a motto of "they shall not pass". It took them seven years (1844–51) to construct a fortress capable of sinking anything that moved. They shipped in granite for the fortifications, had the place bristling with 250 cannons and moved in 500 troops. In 1898 they even mined the waters of the narrow river and set up early versions of torpedoes fired by land lines.

But fortunately or not – depending on which way you look at it – no one with war-like intent has ever come near the place since. Not even close. Last time the guns were fired was to liven up the July 4th celebrations in 1883. Gradually the troops were stood down, the mines disarmed and the mighty guns – capable of firing 42lb hot shot cannon balls – succumbed to rust.

HITCH QUICKS

It's fast everything in America – and getting married is no exception. In Louisiana, you can meet someone on Friday and marry them on Monday. And for just $27.50. One or other of the happy couple, but not necessarily both, takes the cash, birth certificates and any previous divorce decrees, along to get the marriage licence. Then there's just a 72-hour cooling-off period before... ding-a-ling... it's wedding bells. *Info from the Dept of Vital Records in (yes, really) Loyola Avenue, New Orleans.*

TOP SERVICE

Many pubs claim to have something special for working up a thirst. But only one has a roof-top beach volleyball court. It's at the Strathcona Hotel in Victoria, British Columbia, which is now in its third generation of ownership by the sports-mad Olson family. Since Barney Olson bought the place in 1946 it's been turned into a mini-sports center boasting volleyball, a bar called the "Sticky Wicket" crammed with memorabilia for cricket lovers, and a set of lively games rooms.

WHAT'S IN A NAME

You can tell where the Brits have been. About 18 miles north of Quebec City is *Saint-Adolphe-de-Stoneham*, where folk from Gloucestershire settled in the early 1800s. Nearby is *Tewkesbury*. Nowadays the area of forested mountain slopes is popular for skiing in winter with walking and horse-riding in summer. Go another 20 miles west and you find the *Chutes de la Marmite* (yum, yum) – water cascading into potholes on the *Riviere-a-Pierre* in the *Portneuf* wildlife reserve.

SALE OF THE CENTURIES

The world's oldest active retailer is the Hudson's Bay Company. Founded on May 2 1670, it grew rich through the fur and lumber trades in an area of about 4m square kms* of Canada known as Rupert's Land which was granted by England's King Charles II to his cousin Prince Rupert and 17 London merchants. Two centuries later, Rupert's Land was sold to the new Dominion of Canada for £300,000 – although the company kept exclusive trading rights and privileges. These days all HBC's stores have been updated, re-styled and re-badged The Bay or *La Baie*.

(* 4m sq kms is equivalent to roughly 40% of the whole of Canada!)

LOADS OF FUNNY MONEY

Don't laugh. In the UK, a loony is someone who's a bit soft in the head. It's slang for lunatic. In Canada, I wondered why they call their $1 coin a loonie. Now I know. It's nicknamed after the loon, officially described as a "duck-like bird" which was adopted as the Bird of Ontario Province in 1994 and which is featured on the coin's reverse side (to the Queen's head). The loon is a black and white spotted swimming bird which is said to "symbolise the region's unspoiled wilderness, lakes and forests" (sic). There are 5 species of loons worldwide; four of them breed in Canada. The common loon is the most widespread with an estimated 100,000

*Niagara Falls:
15 attempts and five fatalities*

breeding pairs in Ontario where they thrive on fish life in the Great Lakes. They fly fast (120kph or more), dive deep (up to 30m) and make eerie wailing sounds or a "noise like a mirthless laugh" (sic).

* The $2 coin is nick-named a twoonie, although there's a polar bear on the back instead of the bird. *Now that's really loony!*

NIAGARA FALLERS

The first person ever to go over the Niagara Falls in Canada was an over-weight 63-year-old schoolteacher named Annie Taylor. Mrs Taylor, who lied that she was only 43, said she wanted to get rich and famous. She went over in a wooden barrel in 1901 and made a name for herself. But when she died 20 years later she was penniless. Altogether, there have been 15 trips over the 176ft Falls, the last in 1995 by Robert Overacker, a Californian aged 36 whose idea was to jet-ski to the edge and then launch himself off under a rocket-propelled parachute.

ONE WAY or ANOTHER

But it failed to fire, and he plunged to his death. Overacker's was the fifth fatality while two people, Steven Trotter and David Munday, have made the trip successfully twice. Trotter's second time was with his girlfriend. Steel barrels have been the most popular form of recent transport, but there have also been trips in a kayak (fatal) and a "ball" made from rubber tyre tubes (successful). Since the mid-1980s, survivors have been charged and fined under a local law which forbids anyone from performing stunts without permission.

EURO-LANDERS

Ellis Island in the harbour at New York was the official east coast entry point for immigrants to the USA from the 1890s until 1954 when its function was discontinued. Statistics show that in the years of greatest influx (1892–1931) most newcomers came from Italy (2.5m), but the combination of those from Austria-Germany-Hungary topped 3m. There were also 1.9m from Russia and 1m from England/Ireland. All told, 75% of immigrants came from Europe (east and west) during those 40 years.

GOING UP

The world's tallest construction is the CN Tower in Toronto. It stands 1,815ft 5ins and was originally erected to improve TV and communication transmissions over the top of a rash of skyscrapers in the city. The world's tallest building is the Petronas Towers in Kuala Lumpur, Malaysia.

NASDAQ IS VIRTUAL REALITY

All of the USA's financial world – old and new – is represented in New York. On Times Square, in the heart of Manhattan, visitors can see the latest symbol... a video reproduction of an electronic "scoreboard" from the Nasdaq exchange of technology company stock prices. The image is screened onto the outside of a building used by publishers Conde Nast which curves round the corner of 43rd street and Broadway. Unlike the main Stock Market across the city in Wall Street, no physical home actually exists for the

Stock exchange: Steeped in legend

Nasdaq and the giant video billboard is a $20m electronic creation called the Nasdaq MarketSite Experience. Daily trades are actually made through 5,500 terminals around the world to a central computer system in Trumbull, Connecticut, with a backup operation in Rockville, Maryland. Within two years, the plan is for everyone to have direct access to the Nasdaq market either from their home TV screens or through internet equipment.

The New York Stock Exchange, down near the ferry to Statten Island, is at the center of a financial district which is said to generate half of the world's investment capital and is steeped in legend. Close by, is the Museum of American Financial History and the site where Alexander Hamilton, the nation's first Treasury Secretary, had his offices in the 18th century. Money policies set out all those years ago by the popular Mr Hamilton are said still to be the principles on which much of today's US economic system is based. But he wasn't so good with money himself. After an argument about the amorous virtue (or otherwise) of his brother's wife, Hamilton was shot dead in a duel at New Jersey by his rival Aaron Burr. He was aged 49 and – as his surprised executors were soon to find out – virtually penniless. But friends and relatives raised enough money through a special fund to care for his widow and children.

UP YOURS DAD!

Money to found the original Smithsonian Institute in Washington came from an English scientist who never actually went to America. James Smithson was born James Lewis Macie in Paris in 1765. He was an illegitimate son of the widow Elizabeth Macie and her cousin's husband Hugh Smithson, the Duke of Northumberland. It is said that young James was so peeved at not being allowed to inherit his father's title or property (a right he was forced to give up in exchange for becoming a naturalized British citizen) that he vowed to leave any money he made in life to set up "an establishment for the increase and diffusion of knowledge" in America. And he did well. More than $500,000 in gold sovereigns was delivered to America after the chemist and minerologist died in 1829. It paved the way for today's Smithsonian Institute to become the world's largest museum, education and research organisation with 16 museums and galleries in America plus the national zoo and several offshoots overseas. Anthropologists who examined his skeleton in the 1970s came to the conclusion that Smithson smoked a pipe and was only 5ft 6ins tall.

HOME FROM HOME

British Prime Minister Tony Blair today (February 23) meets briefly in Washington with vice-president Dick Cheney before flying off for weekend talks with President George W. Bush at Camp David. Their meeting is held, appropriately, at Blair House, situated in Pennsylvania Avenue just behind the White House. It was once the 19th century home of Francis Blair (no relation), founder and editor of the now-defunct *Washington Globe* (a paper which championed Democratic causes) and friend of Andrew Jackson, America's seventh president and one of its most popular, who put on many lavish receptions at the White House and often invited his friend and neighbour. This century,

President Harry Truman and his family moved into Blair House from 1948–1952 while the White House was undergoing complete structural repairs.

CHEWSY LOT

Americans are eating 1.12billion pounds of popcorn a year, according to the Popcorn Board, a trade organisation in Chicago – and that's not counting all the hot air produced in the "bursting" process which literally pops the corn kernels inside out.

WEEDING OUT THE INVASIVE EXOTICS

Folk in Sarasota, an affluent beach resort on Florida's Gulf of Mexico, have been puzzled to see little flags stuck in flower beds around town like they were marking out holes on a golf course putting green.

The Sunshine State's latest effort at saving our planet is to mark out "non-essential exotic plants" (that's weeds to you and me) for "eradication" (digging up).

'Eradicating the exotics...'
as they beautify Sarasota

ONE WAY or ANOTHER

A notice outside City Hall says: "the city is embracing a philosophy of earth-friendly landscaping." Another explains: "our flowerbeds are being renovated to remove invasive exotic plants, enhance the visual image of downtown, and improve the quality of stormwater run-off which eventually reaches Sarasota Bay."

The way they are doing it is by marking out the good plants (the "native ones") with little green flags, and the weeds (the "invasive exotics") with red ones. Then, they say, they will reduce the exotics by "low-impact maintenance materials and methods" which will not, categorically, include poison or pesticides but will, presumably, include digging out by spade or shovel. Oh, and to help the good ones grow big and strong, yet another sign announces that the garden beds are being sprinkled with "reclaimed water" (rain that's gone through a purifying machine, I suppose).

*At Naples, Sarasota's enviro-friendly rivals further down the coast, an 800yds boardwalk to the beach at Clam Pass is made from 4,320,000 recycled 1gall plastic milk containers.

NAMES IN THE FRAME

Don't be fooled, Niceville hasn't got much going for it. What there is hangs out along a crossroads near Destin, Florida, and it's completely overshadowed by the huge Eglin Air Force base – home, says a very large sign, to the Warriors air strike squadron and, according to a friend of mine who lives nearby, is often visited by B-2 Stealth bombers, those intimidating sci-fly machines which go super-fast on secret missions and look like black manta rays. (Actually, I think she may be a little out-of-date. Someone in the know – quite unofficially of course – tells me the US's latest generation of spy planes is the JSF (Joint Strike Fighter) which is short, dumpy and extremely good at avoiding detection).

Being once a newspaperman, I can't help noticing ones with quirky titles. Here's a couple: The twice-weekly local rag in Venice, Florida, is called *The Gondolier* (what else?) and folk in British Columbia, Canada, have been reading the colourfully-named *Chilliwack Progress* since it was founded in 1891.

Most unusual placename in the world? How about a spot called Head-Smashed-In. Yes, really. It's a place near Lethbridge in Alberta where, 6,000 years ago, native people hunted buffalo to death by driving them over a cliff.

SOMETHING TO GET YOUR TEETH INTO

Sharks hold a macabre fascination for many, mostly fuelled by the movie antics of *Jaws,* the realistic-looking brute they dubbed up at Universal Studios in Hollywood. There are 370 species, according to the excellent display at the Florida Aquarium in Tampa. Some are tiny, like the Lantern and Pygmy at just 6–8ins long, while the biggest, Whale sharks, which can grow to 40ft, are "gentle giants" feeding only on plankton and little fish. Just four types are usually responsible for any attacks on humans – the Great White, Bull, Tiger and Oceanic Whitetip – and only one-third of those attacks are fatal. In 2000, 81 attacks on humans were recorded, of which most (54) were in waters round the USA and the majority of those (35) were off Florida. The state's university at Gainsville has kept official shark attack statistics for years.

It is estimated that 100,000 sharks are caught and killed annually and many types are now endangered species. Florida's fishing laws limit catches to one shark per person per day. Sharks shed their teeth every 2–4 weeks and another set moves forward to replace them, rather like a conveyor belt. A single shark can shed up to 30,000 teeth in a lifetime.

At Venice Beach on the Mexican Gulf fossilised sharks teeth are washed up by the sackfull and local shops will buy them. One family was recently spotted bartering over the price of three large coffee tubs-full

Jaws:
Fake-believe movie shark

ONE WAY or ANOTHER

at *Sea Pleasures and Treasures* in West Venice Avenue, netting $5 per lb for "scrap" (small, low-grade examples) – or they can be bought in packets if you don't happen to find any yourself.

PARTY TIME

The *mardi gras* festival in New Orleans is one of the most famous in the world. It literally means Fat Tuesday (from the French, compris?) and is meant to fall the day before Ash Wednesday when Lent begins. Street processions in the "Big Easy" date from 1872. These days, partying begins at least two weeks before the big parade, and a million visitors turn up for the finale.

AND FINALLY, IT'S PAPA'S PLACE:

Land's End for the USA is, appropriately enough, a T-junction. US Highway 1 (or the Overseas Highway as it is known in the Florida Keys) runs right the way down from Canada to peter out in its last half-mile at Key West, best known as a tourist center and the former haunt of novelist Ernest Hemingway. The road finishes up in Fort Street after which there is only a narrow strip of land where the 19th century Fort Zachary Taylor stood, its ancient cannons pointing out onto the ocean. Within 100yds or so of the very end is Hemingway's house, now a site of national heritage, where the great "Papa" lived with his second wife (of four) between the wars and wrote some of his most famous books on a little typewriter in the upstairs office of a converted outhouse in the garden.

The most southerly point of the States is marked with an old cast-iron buoy, upturned on the sidewalk like a giant thimble and painted in black, red and yellow stripes. Among the information on it, is the fact that Cuba is only 90miles away. In the north, Highway 1 (or Route 1 as it is known up there) hits the Canadian border in Maine at a place called Madawaska – pronounce with a lisp like the island off Africa – before continuing into New Brunswick as Canadian Highway #185.

PASSING THOUGHTS...PASSING THOUGHTS

Key West: End of America

UP TO SCRATCH

The New Zealand name for headlice is coochies.

TOP HOLE

Florida is known as the Sunshine State, but maybe it should be called the Golfers Paradise. It has more golf courses than anywhere else in the USA – 1,200 of them (and more coming at the rate of 50 a year) – and it is estimated nationally, that 1 in every 10 rounds of golf is played there. A superwhizzo World Golf Village has recently opened between St Augustine, said to be the nation's oldest settlement, and Jacksonville.

SIGNS TO REMEMBER

- Along US Highway 8 at Buckeye outside Phoenix, Arizona: "State Penitentiary – do not pick up hitch-hikers."
- Along US Highway 1 at Big Coppitt Key, Florida: "Shark channel – no fishing from bridge."
- Outside lift to skypod viewing platform, another 329ft above the observation deck of Toronto's CN Tower: "Operator is currently elevating guests and will return momentarily – we apologise for the wait."
- Area boarded off for construction of a new "Kids Blast Zone" at Universal Studios, Hollywood: "Pardon the stardust while we enhance our universe."

TAKE NOTE

The nick-name for a US dollar (the buck) is said to have originated from early settlers who reckoned that was the worth of a male deer (a buck) skin.

HOT STUFF

Bois Bande is a Caribbean aphrodisiac and cure for impotence. It's made by taking small pieces of bark from mature bande trees and boiling them with other herbs – but don't ask me why I know...

WHERE'S YOUR MANHOOD?

Poster on a telegraph pole near Harrison's Caves in the parish of St Thomas, Barbados:

All men come and see!
The Men of the Church of God
Welchman Hall, St Thomas
present "Maximize Your Manhood"
a video presentation
by the renowned speaker Dr Myles Monroe
To be held under a tent
at the residence of Bro. Carl Holder
Allen View, St Thomas
on November 28, 2000 at 7.15pm
Come and be enlightened as to what God created you to be
Know the power, purpose and plan of God for Man
Come and learn of your destiny
This is not to be missed!

SIGN OF THE TIMES

Notice in the window of a dusty antiques shop in Greenwich, London. "Opening hours: Monday – sometimes; Tuesday – occasionally; Wednesday – rarely; Thursday – usually; Friday – some afternoons; Saturday – nearly always; Sunday – never." Underneath there is a note: "These times may, and usually do, vary erratically. Please leave a note, or message on answerphone, if you have an inquiry." I wonder if they're still in business?

FANCY THAT

Flying into London on American Airlines, the only place names shown on the seat-back electronic maps for visitors are London (of course)... but Oxford, Brighton and Southampton... really? Also, the only historic sights being highlighted are Runnymede (signing of the Magna Carta) and Chartwell (Churchill's home). Mmmm.

DEAD SERIOUS

Beside the Golden Gate Bridge (which is actually painted "international orange" these days) on the downtown side of San Francisco Bay, there's a graveyard specially for pets. It's a site which the government set up so its servicemen and women could head off to foreign parts happily knowing that if their favourite pooch or parrot passed away in their absence, they would be buried somewhere nice. As well as all the usual dogs and cats, there's even a pet white mouse in there, apparently. Aaaaah.

IT'S ANOTHER LANGUAGE (OR TWO...)

English is the most-used language in the world. But grammar varies hugely (witness spellcheck systems and computer keyboards), and new words are being added all the time. Internationally, there's a completely new vocabulary of computerspeak, like: *program, disk, dot.com, icon, web, e:mail, and log in / off / out...* which are now well-recognised everywhere – but what about the basics?

In America, a "double *l*" often goes missing... as in *travelling, counseling and jewelry* (where the third *e* goes missing, too) and a *c* becomes an *s*, as in *license* (the noun). The *u* is frequently dropped, as in *color, harbor, labor, rumor and tumor,* and unusual, or olde-english, spellings have been simplified as in *tire* (tyre), *lite* (light), *check* (cheque) and *plow* (plough). Elsewhere, when French has influenced the English, the *e* and *r* of words often get transposed, as in *liter* (litre), *meter* (metre), *center* (centre) and *theater* (theatre). Then there's a whole series of commercialistic shortforms: like *stox* (stocks), *x-ing* (crossing), *2-go* (takeaway) and *drive-thru;* plus commonplace slang such as *gotton* (as in: have you got/do you have?), *gonna* (as in: are you going to?), *hella* (as in: hell-of-a-lot-of something) and *outta* (as in: getting out of somewhere/thing). All told, about 4,000 English words are said to be spelled differently – or have different meanings – in America.

In Australia, which has already incorporated many Americanisms into its vocabulary, there's also a whole string of colloquialisms: Here are just a few – *sheila* (woman), *bruce* (man), *sunnies* (sunglasses), *swimmies* (swimming trunks), *flat white* (milky coffee), *bushed* (tired), *crooked* (sick), *billy* (kettle), *stubbie* (small beer bottle), *beaut/dinkum* (pretty), *larrikin* (satirical), *tukker* (food), *swag* (bag), *billabong* (pond), *no worries* (happy), *g'day* (hello), and *possum* (a form of endearment).

BIG MAC

McDonald's is the world's largest fast-food chain. The organisation employs at least 1.5million people and has more than 25,000 restaurants (mostly franchised) in 116 countries. Its staff training programme is bigger than the US Army's.

WOODEN TOPS

The world's tallest trees (coastal redwood), largest (sequoia) and oldest (bristlecone pine), can all be found in California.

TASTY

When foodstuffs manufacturer Fred Walker, an Australian, wanted to launch a product to compete with the ever-popular *Marmite*, he called his brand of yeast-type extract *Pawill* (geddit?). But not many people bought it (or the joke). So he held a competition amongst his customers to find a better name – and someone came up with *Vegemite*, since when, sales have never looked back.

CUMQUAT MAY

When kiwifruits first came to New Zealand from China they were known as chinese gooseberries. But the juicy jobs, which look and taste like sweet cucumber, didn't sell well until 1959 when the NZ ministry for fruit and veg came up with the idea of re-marketing them as Kiwifruits. The rest is history...

DON'T CRY FOR ME...

Was Eva Peron (b. Duarte), wife of the Argentinian dictator, a heroine or a whore? The woman of lowly beginnings who stopped at nothing to get her man, fuelled a revolution and will always be remembered by the songs from West End musicals, died in 1952 aged only 33 from leukemia. But when she was buried among the "high society" of Buenos Aires in the churchyard at Recoleta it nearly caused another revolution. Unknown protestors broke open her tomb and carted the body of their "champion of the working classes" off to Italy for 30 years before relenting, returning the corpse, and having her re-buried.

CASHING IN

The Burj Al Arab hotel in oil-rich Dubai is known as the world's first seven-star hotel. It was built on a man-made island, looks like a giant sail, and costs £2,000 a night to stay in the royal suite.

SPLASH HAPPY

Safety-conscious parents in Palm Beach, Florida campaigned for lifeguards to watch while their kids go paddling in the fountains on city square. From the top of a tennis umpire's chair they sit and survey the toddlers.

Safety-first for the fountains

ONE WAY or ANOTHER

NEW YORK'S DOUBLE VISION

Before that fateful day of September 11 2001, no visit to the financial district of New York's Manhattan was ever complete without a trek up the Twin Towers of the World Trade Center. My trip had taken me there, too, earlier in the year.

The terrorist outrage in which suicide planes decimated both buildings, killing thousands of people and bringing untold misery to the lives of many thousnds more, is already ascribed to history as an event which changed the world.

But could it have been avoided?

All I can say is that on my visit, after not too much more than a perfunctory wave of my Press pass, out came a five-page, closely-typed set of Fact Sheets from the public information people which told more detail than most folk could surely ever want to know about those twin symbols of capitalism which dominated a seven-building, 16-acre site in the heart of the city.

It was only back in 1993 that six people had died there in a bombing attack by terrorists, and I can honestly say I was surprised to be given a set of information with such obvious potential value to someone with evil intent.

Judging in hindsight is always easy. But consider some of this information which was so readily handed to me (I will continue with the present tense):

- 40,000 people work in the Trade Center and more than 150,000 business and leisure visitors turn up each day;

- in the two tower buildings, each floor is approximately one acre in size;

- the floors are column-free and open-plan;

- more than 325 firms and organizations from over 25 countries are represented in the complex;

- they include banking and finance businesses, trade associations, foreign government representation, US Customs, the New York city Board of Trade and various commodity exchanges;

- ten TV stations, including all the major networks, broadcast from the mast atop the Tower One building.

ONE WAY or ANOTHER

South America, Asia & the Pacific

BAG-NAPPED IN ARGENTINA

Buenos Aires, November 9

TODAY I lost a very dear friend. Or, rather, he was kidnapped. It was precisely 3.30 in the afternoon in the ornamental gardens on the square out front of the Casa Rosada, the President's house, in the centre of Buenos Aires.

I am certain of the precise time and location because I reported them later to the police. I also gave them a good description of one of the suspects. He was about 5ft 8 or 9ins, slim, late 30's, short dark curly hair in the Spanish style, shaggy eyebrows, glasses, and wearing an ill-fitting brown wool jacket. He spoke with difficulty; not a lisp, but with an impediment which made him mouth the words softly rather than speak them out loud. I would certainly recognize him again.

As I say, it was a good description. But the cops in the station downtown, only a few blocks away, just shrugged their shoulders in that resigned way, like they do when you know they are only filling in the official report because they have to.

My friend's abduction is not the most important crime they will deal with today. But to me, his loss is central to my very existence. He is my "day-bag" – a zip-off accessory to my main back-pack – which I use for carrying the most immediate necessities. The truth is he was a sale item at a big department store back home. But there is really nothing wrong with him, I assure you.

I would describe him as dark blue, about 18ins high, 12ins wide, and rather bulky. He is a satchel-type, with a collection of zipped pockets and compartments, and adjustable straps which let you slip him neatly over one shoulder if you're on the hoof, or fix on snuggly, like braces, when you are doing some serious travelling. Over the last six months he has been everywhere with me and I shall miss him greatly.

The thieves who made off with him have probably worked the trick a hundred times. The method is as old as the hills. But I still fell for it like a sucker. Casa Rosada (the Pink House) is Argentina's

ONE WAY or ANOTHER

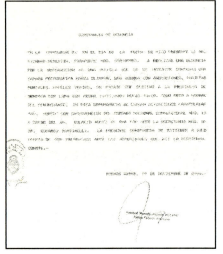

Police statement, typed on an old processor

equivalent of the White House in Washington. It's an attractive colonial building guarded by men in blue, red and white uniforms with hats like they used to wear in history-book pictures, and muskets against their shoulders.

I know the President, Fernando de la Rua, is inside working because two flags fly from the roof, which is the signal. After what happened, I am tempted to write and tell him how poor the security is in his garden.

The square where the kidnap took place was set out nearly 500 years ago. All the important buildings are grouped around it and directly opposite, down the tree-lined Avenida de Mayo, you can see directly to the green-domed parliament.

For tourists like me, it is the No.1 photo opportunity in Buenos Aires; for a couple of *gringos* like them, it is the No.1 thieving attraction.

I have put my bag down on the ornamental flowerbed while I line up a camera shot. There is a tap on my shoulder; I put the camera on top of the bag while I deal with the intrusion. It is the man with the brown jacket and the speech defect. He is asking the way to somewhere. Or, at least, I think he is. To be honest, my Spanish isn't up to much – especially when it comes to understanding those who need some serious oral therapy. But I do my best to help him, and off he goes.

It is merely a diversion, of course – a trick as old as they come. While my back has been turned, my bag has gone; and so has my camera. I do not even catch sight of brown jacket's accomplice. They are both gone. In opposite directions I imagine. No doubt they will meet up later somewhere to examine their spoils from this idiot Englishman.

I am dumbstruck. Incredulous. Staring at the spot where the bag is, or was, or used to be.

A helpful girl is standing not far away. She quickly perceives my distress. Her English is not too bad (well, a lot better than my Spanish anyway). I explain my story. It's not difficult to understand. We go to a policeman on the far side of the square. What can he do? The tourists are feeding the pigeons, a man is selling souvenir flags of Argentina and pictures of the Pink House, families are sitting down on the grass to eat picnics. It's like nothing has happened. But I've been robbed goddamit. Don't you all understand – robbed! I want to scream it out; want them all to know. And the President, too.

The helpful girl's name is Julia de la Cruz. She takes me by the hand. We get on a bus and go to the police station. She is thirty-

Scene of the crime: Out front of the 'Pink House'

ONE WAY or ANOTHER

something, and plump with glasses. She makes a call on her mobile to Standard & Poor, the American finance people, where she works as a clerk. Do they mind if she takes the afternoon off, she is helping a foreign visitor who has been robbed? "No, not at all," they say. It is an adventure for her and she is enjoying it. She is representing Argentina in this international incident. She is apologizing for the behaviour of her fellow countrymen. She is also, as it happens, asking me within half-an-hour if I will marry her. I decline as graciously as I can.

At the police station, as I have said, there is a general shrugging of shoulders at my predicament. It takes three hours. They find someone who can speak English. Several reports are typed out laboriously on an ancient word processor. Then they are signed off by all of us and stamped with official crests. I notice the three, tough-looking cops who are standing nearby with the bulletproof jackets and side pistols, look over in my direction from time to time and break into laughter.

Apart from the kidnap scenario, and the distinguishing marks on my camera, I also list out the contents of my bag: a foolscap size notebook with a hand-written legend on the front which reads *"The travels of Marco Polo Meredith"* and in which I have meticulously recorded the daily events of this trip of mine around the world. To me, it is priceless. To the policeman it is just *el diario* and worth only another shrug of the shoulders.

There is also my contacts book; a hard-covered Filofax affair, in which I have entered the addresses, telephone numbers, FAX and emails of virtually everyone I have ever known. Photographs of family and friends are in another section; pocket-sized maps of the world in another; and useful information on time differences, weight conversion tables, and the best wine vintages in another. What on earth will I do without them, I wonder? And what on earth will the kidnappers do with them?

I suggest to the officer that I might offer a reward of 50 pesos for their recovery. But he is dismissive. "No," he says," I don't think that will be necessary. A miracle is what you need."

In that case then, I think to myself, there seems little point in adding to my list the other things that can be found in my friend's pockets: two packets of spare chewing gum, several boxes of unexposed camera film, some natty wrist-bands which protect you from mosquito bites, a tube of lip salve, and the ending of a roll of toilet paper which I borrowed on a permanent basis from a hotel in New Zealand and which I have been keeping for use in emergencies.

I am also fortunate indeed that on this day, for no particular reason, I did not have my cell phone in the bag, or any spare cash, or my wallet of credit cards and Press pass, or my folder of airline tickets to destinations on this trip of mine which is not quite half completed. On any other day, some or all of them might have been kidnapped too.

But the pain of losing my dear friend is now beginning to overtake me. He has been with me for almost every hour of every day of the six months I have been travelling. He has ridden on my back on the camel that paraded me round the pyramids in Egypt; sat beside me on a train journey that meandered across much of India; went on safari with me into the outback of Australia; up the mountains with me in New Zealand; and "into battle" with me when the army mutinied in Fiji. As a traveller he has been my constant companion, as a journalist he has been my office. And so much more. He has been my library, my comforter. In long waits at airports he has been my pillow; in times of hunger he has provided me with small packets of biscuits.

I shall miss all of him. But the kidnappers will gain nothing from him at all. I imagine them now, opening him up in some dark alley, only to find that it is a clear case of mistaken identity. If they have a conscience they will return him to the scene of their crime. After the police station, I get the bus back there. But he's not on the flowerbed, or abandoned on the grass, or even lying helplessly in one of the waste bins that are dotted around. It's a messy task, but I check them all.

Well maybe he's at the hotel then. Only the other day I tied a label to him on the flight here to Buenos Aires. It says where I am staying. I explain this to the reception people. I show them the statement we made at the police station, point out the official stamps of authority. Don't worry about trying to apprehend *los gringos* if they open the door and chuck him in, I say. If they make a run for it, let them go. I only want my friend back.

They seem to listen to me intently. They make notes for the following shift. I think they consider me English, eccentric and largely insane. But there are no smiles when I key-out the next day, or the next, or the next.

ONE WAY or ANOTHER

It's usually this way, I persuade myself. It's like divorce, or moving house, or a death in the family. There has to be a period of mourning before you can begin again.

I'll wait until Monday. There's a shop on the corner with a daybag in the window. I've already been inside to have a sneaky look at it. It's got more pockets than the other one; and it's a brighter colour, too.

But there's no use thinking that life without my friend will ever be the same, of course.

Postscript

About two weeks later I am leaving Argentina for Los Angeles. At the airport, one of my bags does not go through the security check. I don't know why; there must be some kind of problem in their system. Anyway, I am stopped at the boarding gate and taken away for questioning. My passport has many stamps, maybe they think I am into drugs trafficking? The inquisitors get more and more senior. Already I have missed my plane. Finally, it is the chief of airport security. "So you claim to be a writer, a journalist," he says. "Have you written anything about Argentina?" Yes, I tell him, and I begin to search for a copy of this story you are now reading. "I had my bag stolen. I was in the garden of your President and it..." The man looks up. "My President?" he queries. "Yes," I continue, " Mr de la Rua was in his office and..." The chief of security has heard enough. "I'm so sorry Mr Meredith," he says, "there has obviously been some big mistake. Please come with me and we will get you on the very next flight."

After that there is free coffee and sandwiches, VIP treatment from the airline people, my baggage check-in slip is brought to me personally on the plane by the security staff. All is sweetness and light. Was I economical with the truth? Well OK. But Mr de la Rua is a politician; I'm sure he would understand.

© Richard Meredith & Mercury Books – all rights reserved

GUNFIGHT IN PARADISE

Chapter 1
Journalists are born, not made

Vitu Levu, Fiji; November

THERE has always been a debate within journalism over whether it should be called a profession. Those who make the rules on these things, who administrate, set the standards, organize training, or generally want to regularize it all, will always say that it is. But I'm not so sure. How, after all, do you include "rat-like cunning" as a necessary qualification in a learned profession?

Nicholas Tomlin of the *Sunday Times*, who was so tragically and prematurely killed while covering the Middle East conflict in the 1970s, included the "cunning" sobriquet when asked to define the qualities of a good journalist. Maybe a "calling" – more usually applied to those who follow a religious vocation – would be better. There is no academic qualification which teaches you to dare to go where others dare not, in hot pursuit of a good story. Or what it is inside you that makes you want to be first on the scene if there is likely to be an "exclusive" to be had.

I haven't always been a journalist. There was a time after school when I flirted with accountancy. My father, who had established a profitable practice of private clients in the licensed trade, wanted me to take it on from him with one of my brothers. But office work wasn't for me, and one day I shocked them all by saying that I was packing it in and going abroad. "Where?" asked my mother in some confusion. "Don't know, "I said, "Europe probably." Forward planning isn't a phrase you come across much when you are a teenager.

"How long will you be away for?" mother continued. "Not sure. I'll just see how I get on."

And that's how it was. I was 19, I put a kit-bag over my shoulder, £40 in my pocket, and stuck my thumb out for a lift to Dover. I didn't come back for a year, and I had the most wonderful, adventurous time travelling my way across France, Spain,

ONE WAY or ANOTHER

Switzerland, Belgium, Germany and Holland.

My father ("Pop" to all of us young ones in the family) gave me a letter to stick in my back pocket promising "whomever it may concern" that he would pay my passage home from anywhere in the world in case of an emergency. I never needed it, but it was a nice feeling to know that it was there. I found work as I went. Car cleaner in a garage, house boy, butcher's boy, waiter, kitchen hand. In Amsterdam, I even sold watercolour paintings. They were amateurish and appalling, but the generous Dutch, who have a proud tradition of encouraging art, still happily handed over a few guilders after I had "pitched" them on their front doorsteps.

It was a magical year. I met some fascinating people, visited some fabulous places, and paid my way as I travelled. I only used buses or trains or my thumb to get myself around. I slept on the floor in friends' apartments, under boats on the beach, and once or twice in posh hotels. Some days I would survive for 24 hours on a packet of biscuits. Once I was treated, with my girlfriend, to a five-course meal in a swanky Parisian restaurant by a wealthy Frenchman with a Mercedes. She departed with him the next day.

It was my first taste of travelling – so distinctly different from holiday-making – and I loved every minute of it. It was the reason I became a journalist.

There was no email or electronic gadgetry in those days. Phone calls were only for emergencies. It was down to the trusty old pen and paper as I recounted my adventures to family and friends, and it wasn't long before they were suggesting that I try my hand at writing for a living.

Now, like I say, I reckon that journalism is more of a calling than a profession. I also happen to think that good journalists are born and not made.

Rat-like cunning is certainly one of the qualifications. Others, I would suggest, include a natural inquisitiveness, good observation and memory, perseverance, and a strong nerve (or downright cheek). None of them are exactly text-book material. There is also that illusive factor called Luck – which, depending on what you believe about these things, you either make for yourself or which is made for you.

My grandfather Harry used to say the "damn thing" was in your blood. Poor Harry, I really only got to know him in his last few years. He was a victim, like countless thousands of others, of the inhuman gas weaponry of World War 1. He had worked on the *Evening Standard* in London, but the gas eventually did for him, destroying his eyesight and undermining his gifted brain, which had once earned him the reputation as something of a mathematical genius.

My father Jack, the accountant, was devoted to the *Daily* and *Sunday Express*. When I was growing up, the old "Crusader" was the big paper for middle-class Britain. For millions like my "Pop", the Canadian Lord Beaverbook's personal and editorial support of Churchill in World War II, earned the paper a special loyalty. It said the things they wanted to hear which, like John Junor's popular column on Sundays, was gung-ho and (in today's climate) politically incorrect. In its heyday, the daily's circulation was more than 4m – a great many people – and it made them listen.

Imagine then my bright-eyed wonder, as within five years of returning from that hitch-hiking jaunt around Europe, I should find myself being taken onto the payroll at the imposingly-shiny, black glassed offices of the *Daily Express* in Fleet Street, London.

I had done well. Alan Booth, editor of my local weekly newspaper, listened earnestly to the stories of my foreign adventures, and decided to take me on as a trainee. In three years I had a chief reporter's job and a name for uncovering the unusual, and even the unpalatable, in sleepy, suburban St Albans.

Next there was a spell with the *Evening Echo* at Hemel Hempstead, also launched by a Canadian (Lord Thomson), and where, being a daily, it was really drummed into me that, in the news business, it is always best to be first. I was lucky, too, to be working in the company of a fine young set of writers like Anthony Holden, Stephen Pile and John Coldstream who went on to make their names as authors and/or national newspaper columnists.

At the *Daily Express*, my own career began to take a different course. Marriage and the responsibilities of fatherhood persuaded me to "come indoors" and I became a sub-editor with the news department team, pulling together in-coming copy from our staff reporters, correspondents and agencies on some of the major stories of the day at home and abroad. We had to work quickly, but we had to stay calm. There were big signs suspended from the ceiling all around our offices. "Make it fast, make it accurate," they said. I have never forgotten them.

In the newspaper business, a national like the *Express* is, of course, Premier Division stuff. Our editing team was entrusted with the copy of "star" writers of the day – like Chapman Pincher, the legendary Defence Correspondent, who was said to have had better sources inside MI6, the secret military intelligence service, than the Prime Minister. There was also Jean Rook, the fiery Women's Editor, who did as much as anyone to put the F into modern Feminism.

We knew the meaning of "world exclusive" too; Martin Borman, the notorious Nazi war criminal, being "discovered" in South America by one of our reporters (although, in fact, the man later turned out to be a Peruvian milkman); Ronnie Biggs, the Great Train Robber, spilling out his story from a hideaway in Rio; Lord Lucan (or was it?) being spotted on the run in the scandalous nanny-murder case.

On big "scoops" like these we were sworn to secrecy. No careless talk by us "subs" in the pub where our rivals might overhear. The "comps"– the compositors who set the type – had to keep their traps shut, too. Proofs of pages were locked away, and they stayed that way until the first edition came out.

Then there would be the most almighty scramble in the opposition camps as they tried to cobble together something of their own to "save face". It was competitive, exciting, sometimes farcical, but always a thrill. As I've said, in the newspaper business which I had come to love, Rule No1 is: To be first is to be best.

But that was then and this is now. For me, it seems a long time since those heady days of Fleet Street. Even then, the long decline of the *Daily Express* had begun. Circulation has fallen dramatically and continuously to around 1m as middle-class Britain has switched allegiance to the more lively *Daily Mail* and the populist *Sun*. There have been changes of owners and changes of editors but the spiral seems inexorable. In this Age of Brand Names, few would argue that the *Daily Express* still counts for something, but – to use one of those typical newspaper-style clichés – it has become a Shadow of Its Former Self.

I left because I wanted to get into publishing. After two businesses of launching and running newspapers, magazines and, lately, electronic publications, I have had to learn the skills of organizing, marketing, finance and administration. But the roots

GUNFIGHT IN PARADISE

Paradise at Sigatoka, where the author stayed

run deep. I have never lost that ambition to "chase after fire engines"; not changed my character, not changed my blood.

I tell you these things now because of what happened during 24 hours this week while I was in the South Pacific "paradise" of Fiji. Danger, excitement, a "scoop", and the *Daily Express*... they all came together for me once again.

Chapter 2
Exclusive! Mutiny at the barracks

JOURNALISTS are a close-knit bunch. It's a small industry. You get to know who's who. You keep friends and contacts. You maintain loyalties.

I have sold my business, put a few pennies in the bank, decided to take 12 months off to see the world – as a traveller again, not as a holidaymaker – and I am writing as I go. Mostly it's been feature articles about the places I've been or the things that I've done. One day, I hope to get them published in a book; a kind of travellers' companion.

Occasionally there have been newsworthy pieces. I went, for example, to Indonesia where the genocidist former president Haji Mohammad Suharto, was due to stand trial. In the event, after a string of doctors testified that he was too ill, it didn't happen. But I still filed a "background" piece to Tim Shipman, acting Foreign Editor of the *Daily Express*.

ONE WAY or ANOTHER

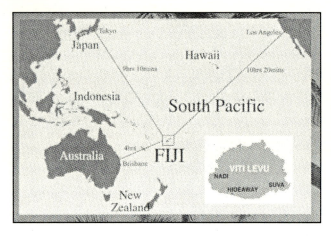

Fiji's island nation in the South Pacific

He liked it. "Where else are you going on this trip of yours?" he asked. I started to run through the list; Australia, New Zealand, Fiji... "Ah, Fiji," he said, "now you might find some news there." We all knew how a botched coup, earlier in the year, had made headline news around the world. Trouble in the tropics, shootings, hostages being held for nearly two months, strong British connections... "Things are tight (financially) here," said Tim. "We can't ask you to go. But you could keep an eye on things for us if you're going anyway."

"Of course," I agreed. "No problem." Old loyalties, like I say.

Now call it co-incidence, luck or whatever, but by the time my visit to Fiji arrives, a number of things are already on the agenda. George Speight, leader of the failed coup, is about to be tried for treason; the annual summit of South Pacific nations is to be held on nearby Kiribati, and the Fijians will be "celebrating" 30 years of independence from Britain. I Fax Tim: "It's got the makings of a pretty good punch-up," I suggest. Little did I realise...

I am flying to Fiji from Auckland, New Zealand. Before I go, my brother Nick, who was once a pilot of Tornado fighter-bombers in the RAF, advises me to check on the current situation with the British Consulate. One of those middle-aged ladies who will always do their duty for Queen and Country prints me off the latest Travel Advice. "There is a continuing risk of civil unrest," it says. It also advises all visitors to Fiji to register with the British High Commission in Suva, the capital. I look through the small print at the bottom. Any person who republishes information

GUNFIGHT IN PARADISE

from this Travel Advice notice will be liable to prosecution, it says. How ridiculously British! Better not tell anyone else then.

It doesn't take me long to find out that all is indeed not well in paradise. I am on Vitu Levu, the largest island in Fiji, which is itself a scattered nation of more than 300, mostly volcanic, islands. Two hours by rickety bus from my beachside hotel and I am in Suva.

Today is *Dwali*, the annual holiday festival of the islands' large Indian community, but no one is celebrating, the shops are shut and everyone is staying at home. At the local radio station, the army has just released three journalists who they took away for questioning. I get to see one, the director of news. But she is too frightened to talk. Then I go to the British High Commission.

It is, appropriately enough, in Gladstone Road. A sign outside says that they close on Fridays at noon. It is Friday. It is 12.30pm. They are closed. Sammy, the security guard, spots me peering at the notice and makes my acquaintance. He is a smiling man. He is sorry, but there is not much he can do. I write down my name and that I am a journalist and where I am staying and give him the piece of paper to hand into the office when it re-opens. That's it then, I have registered my presence. Brother Nick would be pleased.

Indian-owned shop burned out in the May riots

ONE WAY or ANOTHER

Thursday, November 2
3.07pm local (4.07am Weds, GMT)

I file a completed feature article by e-mail to Geoff Compton, my contact on the *Daily Express* in London. There is such a feeling of foreboding about this place. Speight's trial has been put off, but Odgie (whom I have nick-named "dodgy" Odgie) who is a security guard at the hotel complex and – importantly – who also knows that I am a journalist, has invited me to a secret meeting with some islanders tomorrow.

They are mad for rugby here. Odgie is a fan. I used to play a lot. We get on well. He tells me things. I'm sure something is about to blow. But what? Best to get the ball rolling with something across to London then.

My story is about the money problems all this unrest is causing. Nothing too sensational, but it's not bad, and it will show them I've done my homework. The article begins:

"The Queen's face is still on the banknotes, but the currency is close to going broke in paradise..." (see appendix–1)

3.15pm local (4.15am Weds, GMT)

The wife of the hotel owner tells me the radio is reporting that shooting has started in the army barracks at Suva. "Fire-fight apparently broken out. I'm on my way to find out more," I Fax to London and refer them to my earlier story, sent less than ten minutes ago.

So here we go again; being a reporter once more, feeling that adrenaline rush. "To be first is to be best." Remember? It's in the blood.

I put on what I call my "battle dress" – jeans, loose shirt, lots of pockets. The "day–bag" goes over my shoulder. Inside it: camera, mobile phone, contacts book, notepad, wallet, money, credit cards, Press ID. My passport goes in a neat little pouch that hangs from my belt and tucks inside my trousers.

Local knowledge is ahead of me. Dodgy Odgie has already heard that there is to be a curfew imposed on Suva at 6pm. I wonder why I can't get a taxi; not at any price. Now I know. It's 4.30pm and it's two hours to Suva. They would never get back. There's only one thing to do... I go out to the road and flag down the first car.

GUNFIGHT IN PARADISE

Now this is where fate lends a hand; and not for the only time in the next 24 hours either. Katrina Barclay and Chris Koentges are a young couple on holiday from Calgary in Canada. They are startled; but at least they understand my quick explanation. Not only that, but he's a writer and she's studying communications at college back home. Within minutes they are as up for this adventure as I am! Can they deliver me to Suva before the roadblocks and the curfew shutters come down at 6pm? Chris puts his foot down.

We make it, with minutes to spare.

First I go to the Centra Hotel which as the name suggests, is central for most things in the capital. It is also the place where most of the journalists hung out while Speight's attempted coup was going on. Renadi, the loftily-titled Guest Relations Officer at my holiday place, knows the receptionist here very well. She has scribbled her a note: "Asilika, please help Mr Meredith (Richard) UK journalist." I quickly get an update from her:

First this is serious: There's apparently been a mutiny at the barracks with two dead already and several wounded;

Second, the curfew at 6pm is not only for public transport – but everyone must be off the streets by 8pm or they could be shot;

Third, the Centra Hotel is one of the very few places in town to have internet facilities. Phew!

We get hold of a taxi driver who's willing to take me up to the barracks. His name is Novelli. He's a local lad with the twinkle of devilment in his eye and a pretty good idea of what's going on. As we pass along streets confused with traffic, an announcement comes on the radio that the shooting's stopped and the trouble is over. But I'm not so sure. And nor is he.

How right we were! The Queen Elizabeth II Barracks is on a hill on the outskirts of town. The army has got it sealed off; or, at least, they think they have. But Novelli knows differently. It takes him half an hour to find the little service road that not many people know about which leads down to the camp from behind a row of shops. We have a bird's-eye view.

No more shooting? You must be joking! Just down below us all hell is still breaking loose. The deadly chatter of machine-gun fire, single cracks of pistol shots and, from time to time, the big thump of an exploding grenade.

In the darkness it's difficult to make out – as it must be for the

ONE WAY or ANOTHER

protagonists – just who is where amongst the trees and the buildings of the spread out barracks which is the central base for Fiji's army of several hundred soldiers. I can hear the whine of ricocheting bullets ('tho fortunately not often in our direction) and I calculate that the gun battle has been going on for five hours. The casualty toll will be high.

"Right," I tell Novelli. "I've seen enough. We've got half an hour left. Let's go and see if we can get some facts about what's happening."

The Ministry of Information is a substantial pile of grey-block offices in the middle of town. We arrive there after a wild-goose chase to the police HQ where they refuse to sanction a curfew pass no matter how much fuss I make. With just 10 minutes left, it is now-or-never to get some kind of result from the Ministry. The gaggle of policemen and armed soldiers at the doors of the building bar my way. But something in my babble about "world news... journalist from London... *Daily Express*..." must have done the trick. For within a couple of minutes I am being ushered down the corridor and into the private office of the Director of Information.

Eliki Bomani looks the harassed man that he so obviously is. His desk is crowded with papers, he is busy feeding his fax machine with hand-written messages, and the phone is a constant interruption. Yet to his eternal credit, he stops the lot while I get out my notebook and he answers my questions for 10 long minutes. Now I get the full story – or the "official" version of it at least – for the first time: There has indeed been a mutiny at the barracks; about 20 (to be confirmed) rebel soldiers loyal to Speight have tried to capture/kill the head of the Armed Forces. But he has escaped; they have raided the armoury and taken machine guns and rocket-propelled grenades; they are from the CRW (Counter Revolutionary Warfare) unit. Some of them have been British-trained at Sandhurst and Camberley; there are 11 casualties to date including two dead; loyal troops have now repulsed and surrounded them, but they are holding five people hostage including a civilian.

Not a bad story eh? Not for any journalist; especially one with all those born-not-made things in his blood.

Mr Bomani continues: "The situation has quietened down now. In fact, several of the rebels have given themselves up." Ahem, I am able to interrupt. "Sir, I have just come from the barracks myself and I would say that you still have quite a battle on your hands." He looks shocked at this. "Oh, have you really? Well maybe there's a little more mopping up to do."

I can see that my eye-witness knowledge has given me some respect.

The Fax machine starts to hum again. It is a draft from the Prime Minister of a speech he wants to put out on TV. Mr Bomani hands it to me. "What do you think?" Now the phone is going again. It's the *BBC* – "your *BBC*," he says with grin – before taking the call. And now he is writing his personal mobile number on his business card for me. "Use this to get yourselves a curfew pass and call me if you need any help." It works, too. Back at the police station the boss eats humble pie.

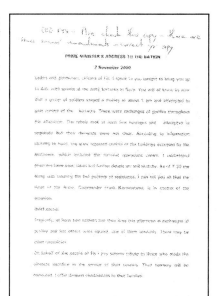

Draft of PM's TV message

My next port of call is the hotel internet machine. There's a message from Geoff Compton at the *Express*. He's got my earlier feature about Fiji and he's passed it to Jacqui Goddard who is standing in for Tim Shipman (gone to cover the presidential election in the States). He will also pass on anything else I file.

Geoff has taken time, too, to fill me in with some new gossip about the future of the *Express*. "The latest bidder is, would you believe, the *Mail*," he says. I e-mail (and Fax him too, for good measure) the first of my stories about today's fighting:

8.52pm local (9.52am Thurs, GMT)

"Two soldiers have been killed and at least 10 others injured in a mutiny at Fiji's national army barracks outside the capital Suva. Gunfire is still being heard from the Queen Elizabeth II barracks tonight (8pm local)..."

ONE WAY or ANOTHER

What luck, I am thinking to myself: A hot news exclusive for the *Express* – a first-hand report from the only foreign journalist on the spot and a good background feature already on the desk in London to back it up. Even the timing has been fortunate. It's the start of the day over there. They will have lots of time to source some pictures, give it to the graphics people, make a real spread of it! As the night wears on, I file again:

Friday, November 3
12.20am local (1.20pm Thurs, GMT)

"FOUR soldiers now dead in Fiji and up to 19 injured including eight civilians. Approx 20 armed rebels from the crack Counter Revolutionary Warfare Unit are said to have escaped the barracks blockade by loyal troops..."

No one's going to get much sleep tonight, but when the adrenaline is pumping, who cares? I snatch some rest here and there but too much is happening to switch off. By early morning the story has developed further and I can file again to London:

8.45am local (9.45pm Thurs, GMT)

"EIGHT soldiers are now known to have died in last night's mutiny at the Queen Elizabeth II army barracks in Suva, Fiji. Another 21 are in hospital plus seven civilians hit by stray bullets.
 Through the night loyal forces have been hunting for around 20 armed rebels who escaped when their attempted takeover apparently failed, a further 20 are under arrest..."

It's been a long night, but I am elated. What a cracking story; the kind of live action story that most journalist's would give their right arm for. The later edition deadlines will be looming in London; I figure it's time I gave the Foreign Desk a call to see if they need anything else.
 "Is Jacqui there?" I ask. "Who's this?" says the voice. "It's Richard Meredith calling you from Fiji."
 "Oh; no, I'm afraid she's gone home now."
 "Ah, well who am I speaking to then?"
 "It's Nick Flemming," says the voice. "Can I help?"
 "Well Nick, it's just that I've been filing all this stuff about the

mutiny here, and I wanted to know if you needed anything more."

"You'll have to forgive me," says Nick, "but I've only just come on and I'm honestly not quite sure what we've got in the paper tomorrow. Give me five minutes and I'll call you back."

The phone goes. "Look I'm sorry," says Nick, "I've checked, but we are not running anything on Fiji. I can say that categorically."

"What nothing…?" I blurt out. "Good God! Well, Fiji obviously doesn't count as an item of interest to readers of the *Express* any more."

"I'm sorry," says Nick. "You know how it is, but I'm afraid I don't make the agenda…"

I put the phone down slowly. Stare at it. Still can't believe it. Can this really be the same daily "Crusader" which was once the pinnacle of my ambition and the inspiration of my peers and colleagues? I am stunned.

Another journalist has arrived. The first non-local to join me on the story is Sean Dawney. *Associated Press's* radio man has got to the hotel through the curfew with the official party back from the South Pacific summit. "I bet you had quite a night last night," he chides me with envy in his voice. I reel off all the facts and details. "Wow, what a good yarn," he says.

"But do you know what?" I exclaim, "London's just told me they're not using it."

"You're joking! It's a cracking story. And all those British connections here too…"

"Tell me about it," I say dejectedly.

Chapter 3
Running the gauntlet with Bull-neck

Friday, November 3
10am local

WITH 15 armed, desperate soldiers still being hunted in the streets of Suva, the Fiji authorities announce, not surprisingly, that last night's curfew will continue all day. No one and nothing but essential services will be able to move around. It is effectively cut off; a ghost town.

In London, it is the middle of the night now – but in any case I

ONE WAY or ANOTHER

feel so deflated by the *Express* that I don't consider I would do anything more for them even if I got the exclusive story that World War III was breaking out.

Michael Holland and his camera crew from *Television New Zealand* have driven through the night to get here and bluffed their way through the roadblocks. They, too, are flabbergasted that the *Express* hasn't touched the story. It has been the second lead item (after the Middle East's new flare-up) on the *BBC World News*, they tell me.

"Well, I'll leave the buggers to it then," I say – and I begin, instead, to start thinking about how I can get myself out of here and back to my holiday.

The hotel lobby, now that the full extent of the crisis has become apparent, is milling with an odd mixture of people. It's a strange thing when a crisis overtakes a country which gets much of its income from tourism. Just two or three months back while there were riots going on in Indonesia and the world was learning the full extent of its president's evil rule in East Timor, life was carrying on as normal in Bali, the country's tourist enclave.

Here at the comfortable Centra Hotel in deserted Suva, holidaymakers still lounge by the pool or play football with their kids while the army is driving around the empty streets outside looking to kill their former colleagues, the leader of whom, it is now emerging, is a captain with the very British-sounding name of Shane Stevens.

In the lobby, non-tourist residents are taking things more seriously. Harassed reps, unable to make their visits, are on their mobiles to head office asking for instructions; myopic Japanese businessmen are taking pictures of anything and everything; fat Americans sit in large armchairs holding court to anyone who'll listen; some folk are badgering the management to get them passes (until it becomes known that hundreds of people are queuing at the police station downtown claiming to be part of an essential service); others have just resigned themselves to watching TV and waiting for the crisis to blow over – or develop.

I have made some phone calls to try and find someone to get me out of here. But when was a taxi ever essential transport?

And why should a journalist be an acceptable form of life one day when they have been arresting them even before this shooting began?

GUNFIGHT IN PARADISE

At one stage I set off, either bravely or foolishly, to walk to the Ministry of Information. Mr Bomani, the so-helpful Director from last night, is now unobtainable by phone. As I get near the offices, several soldiers appear from behind trees and buildings to bar my way and brandish their rifles. They are a jittery lot. But who wouldn't be when the only person they might expect to appear is a former colleague who now wants to kill them? No good there then.

Just as I get back to the hotel there is a sudden commotion as two smoke-glassed Toyota wagons draw up in a rush. It's the Prime Minister, someone says. The New Zealand TV crew get ready for action as a collection of men get out.

Mr Bomani's number now became unobtainable

"Which one is he?" I hear the cameraman ask.

Laisenia Qarase is a tall, bespectacled, grey-haired fellow who is a banker by profession. A quietly-spoken, moderate man, he has been appointed (not elected) to "hold the fort" since the May coup and to keep things as calm as possible until full democracy can be restored.

Maybe that's the problem, he is too mild-mannered to cope with Fiji's difficulties. Dressed conservatively in grey jacket and matching grey sulu, the traditional kilt-like skirt which, I am told, was "invented" by a previous Fijian politician when he came back from studying at Oxford in the 1940s, he is quickly ushered upstairs for a pre-cabinet briefing.

A demure, willowy blonde goes with him. We realize she has been waiting there in the lobby for his arrival. "Who is she?"

"Oh no, not another sex scandal," says Sean, the *AP* man. But I don't think so. When we button-hole her afterwards she says she is just a family friend. And we believe her. She isn't the type.

I try to talk to Mr Qarase as he is bustled out, but now is not the time, he says diplomatically. "Well how about a lift," I am tempted to say. Several large men with square shoulders persuade me that now is not the time to ask that question either.

ONE WAY or ANOTHER

2.00 pm local time

My break-through comes. No one is getting around outside. No one is driving up to the hotel unless it is the Prime Minister or an armoured truck or an essential service vehicle. No one that is, except Mr X (I am never given his name for obvious reasons, as you will see). He just seemed to appear from nowhere through the front doors. I can hardly say he ghosted in – because he is built like a tank.

Many Fiji men look in good physical shape. Maybe it's the warrior in them. They make good soldiers; they make good rugby players. The young ones stand about 6ft 2 or 3ins with close-cropped hair and mahogany skins. Mr X was once like that, I imagine. But now he is approaching 40 (I guess), his head is shaven, his neck is like a bull's, and his belly bulges out under his T-shirt. He seems to know who I am. And I'm not arguing.

"You want to get back to Sigatoka," says Bull-neck. It is a statement, not a question. "It will cost you F$50 (£17)." The money's no problem, I say, but what about the curfew? "Don't you worry; we are going to a funeral," he says.

In the car he produces a piece of paper. I can't read it, but Bull-neck says it is a pass which gives him permission to go to a funeral. Novelli, my driver from last night, knew I would want to get about today. His friend with the big belly needs the money. The funeral is a scam and he got the pass through a soldier pal. "I'll just say you are my friend and you are coming to the funeral with me," he says. I don't argue with that either.

It takes nearly an hour to get out of town. We run the gauntlet through four checkpoints. At each of them, the road is cordoned off with a variety of barricades and spiky contraptions that blow your tires out if you fail to stop. Soldiers and policemen, but mostly soldiers, swarm about with weapons cocked and ready. There are 15 of their former colleagues out and about and who-shoots-first could mean the difference between life and death.

Each time, they make Bull-neck get out with his piece of paper and explain his story. He is really earning his money. Usually, a couple of them peer in through the window at me. Thank you God for giving me fair hair and a white complexion. No way can I be a Fijian army rebel on the run.

They search Bull-neck, they search inside the car, they search the boot, but no one bothers to search the day-bag over my shoulder

GUNFIGHT IN PARADISE

with all my journalist's paraphernalia inside. And no one finds my wallet with the Press ID tucked inside with the Visa and American Express cards."

"Why did you risk all that," I ask Bull-neck as we finally pull clear of the town and bump our way along the winding coastal road in his battered old car. "I need the money," he says, "it's my daughter's birthday today. Now I can buy her a present."

We are out of danger. Things start to loosen up a little. He knows who I am – or rather what I am – and he wants to know what I make of it all. And I, of course, being what I am, want to know what he knows, too. It's a surprising amount.

No way to check it all out I'm afraid, but Bull-neck is tough all right – 15 years around the world with merchant ships have seen to that – and he knows a thing or two about "the troubles".

Togetherness can work: A Fijian and an Indian stroll in Suva

"What a bungle they made of it last night," he says. "Fancy missing the opportunity of killing the army chief. Do you know where he is today?" I said I didn't.

"They've put him on a ship and sent it sailing round to keep him out of the way." M'm, this fellow does know a bit...

"And why on earth did they do it on a Thursday?" he continues. I shrug my shoulders. "It would have been so much better on a Wednesday – that's sports day at the camp. Everyone would have been down at the sports field. It would have been easy."

I ask Bull-neck if he has ever met George Speight. He said he had. "He's a great talker," he says, "and, sure enough, he knows what all our problems are – but he doesn't have any solutions."

What are your problems? I prompt the big man. He pours it out. The bottom line is all about Indian immigrants buying or taking over land which the native Fijians consider to be theirs.

His argument is racist and blatantly "politically incorrect" in today's world. But then when you've just risked your life for your daughter's birthday party, I guess that doesn't matter much.

And what's going to happen now? I prompt again. "Well it isn't all going to go away after last night's fighting," he says. "A great many Fiji people want to do battle for what we think is ours."

But first, he adds, they will have to catch the ones who got away. "If they catch them, they will kill them; you'll see," he says.

"Last time, in the coup, some of them got away too. But I saw the soldiers catch one of them in a garden as I was driving past. They clubbed him with their rifles until he was dead. The police just stood there watching – and so did a little girl like mine. Ten years old. Can you imagine?"

There's no time for more conversation. Here comes my hotel after the long drive back. I hand over the F$50. In all the circumstances, it's been a real bargain.

"I hope your daughter has a very happy birthday," I say.

Several people come out to meet me.

I look at my watch – it's 4pm; almost exactly 24 hours since I walked out onto this same piece of road and waved down the Canadians. One or two things have happened since then...

Postscript

1. Night of Friday, Nov 3: Soldiers find Alifereti Nimacere, who was implicated in the May coup, and club him to death.
2. Nov 9: Geoff Compton of the *Express* answers my "what happened?" question. "Frankly, your guess is as good as mine," he says.
3. Late Nov: *Express Newspapers* are sold to Richard Desmond, publisher, among other things, of *OK!* the celebrity magazine, and *Penthouse*, for £125m
4. April 19: Speight is brought from his prison island of Nukulau to be told that his trial will start in June and could last three months. A general election to form a new government will be held on August 27.

© Richard Meredith & Mercury Books – all rights reserved

Also see Appendix-1

JUST CALL ME FRANK

Queenstown, New Zealand; October

WE USED to play it as kids. Maybe you still do. It's just the job for long journeys in the car.

You know the thing. Everyone has to look out for pub names as you go along. One point for a colour, two for an arm, three for a leg. It works well in the UK, of course, where there are so many pubs. "Nice one" – for the *Black Swan* (7 points); "Yippee" – for the *George and Dragon* (22); "Yabadabadoo" – for the *Charge of The Light Brigade* (game over!!).

But here's a tip: Don't ever play the Name Game down the West Coast of New Zealand's *South Island*. You'll never keep track of the points.

The place is pure picture postcard stuff. Hidden valleys, lush green rainforests, snow-capped mountains, mirror-glass lakes. It's a World Heritage Site. Nature has bestowed more of its majestic gifts along here than virtually anywhere else.

And Man has made his contribution, too. There are more road signs than you can shake a stick at. If ogling all this out-of-this-world scenery isn't enough, you can have yourself the highest-scoring game of I-spy in the universe.

I had come across from *Christchurch* in the east on the wonderful railway – one of the world's Top 6 for mountain-spotting – that traverses the island up over *Arthur's Pass*. A hired car at *Greymouth*, and now there was a straight run down the coast on the western side.

The Name Game bug first bit me that evening. Driving in the rain and descending darkness, they loomed up so often in the headlights it was just impossible to miss them.

I was heading for *Fox's Glacier* and the nearby *Lake Matheson*, two of New Zealand's most famous natural attractions. The signs caught my eye all the way along. Yellow rectangles with black lettering. There were scores of them. *Smithy's Creek, Kiwi Jack's, Gillespie's Point*... it got me thinking about I-spy.

ONE WAY or ANOTHER

The signs were marking out all the gulleys and the creeks and the culverts where the water comes pouring off the mountains, disappearing under the road, and then rushing down towards the sea. So many of them. Such evocative names. But what did they all mean?

This morning, with the sun now thankfully restored, I carry on my journey down the coastal highway between the veggie-green *Tasman Sea* and the rugged *Southern Alps*. And now I am looking for them. Jotting them down. Totting up the points. No nameless wonders here.

This land once belonged only to the Maoris. Still does, in a manner of speaking. They got first call on naming names.

One legend has it that water rushes down the mountains everywhere here because the great Maori god *Tue Te Rakiwhanoa* envisioned the *Alps* as a giant canoe filling up with water. So he broke down bits of the side to let the water out and stop the island from capsizing.

Another is that the lakes were formed from the tears of the Maori goddess *Hinemoa* who saw her lover fall to his death while they were out climbing.

The children that came after them gave the rivers and lakes their names: Angry, swirling rivers called *Hokitika, Wanganui, Manakaiaua and Macarora*; and giant, ice-grey lakes called *Kariere, Mapoueika, Paringa and Moeraki*.

Not being too well up on the Maori language, I honestly can't tell you whether their names are worth a shed load of points. But I can tell you why Anglo Saxon man came to leave so many of his marks along this coast. It was all down to a gold rush. I looked it up in the library.

Come the 1860s, these *Westlands* were teeming with prospectors, many of them British; early settlers hoping to find their fortune in the land that was billed as, quite literally, the "Last Place on Earth". Someone spotted the glint of gold in the streams gushing off the Alps and word spread faster than you can say *Big Nugget*.

I once remember travelling up the west coast of Eire. Same kind of thing – lots of names with colourful connections. There was *Kitty O'Shea's* wine cellar, *Trixie Pat's* piano pub, *Frank Mahoney's* bottle bar... but that wasn't a patch on this. Not from here to *Tipperary* it wasn't.

JUST CALL ME FRANK

*Lake Paringa:
Named by the Maoris*

It really is extraordinary. From the famous *Fox's Glacier*, where as you would expect, there's a mint of signs, right down to the *Haast Pass* (about 150 kms or so), I swear there must a hundred of those yellow and black nameboards.

No points for descriptive ones like *Thirsty Culvert*. Or creeks like *Windbag, Dismal, Dizzy, Boulder* or *Spout*.

Odd ones like *Bishop's Folly, Roaring Swine* and *Doughboy's Creek* might cause a back-seat argument. But it's the gold prospectors who panned out their lives all those years ago who score the best. Two for an arm, three for a leg, remember? That's 10 per person if you get my point. So thank you *Dusty Miller, Dick, Potter, Murphy* and *Jamie* for giving your names to the creeks where you toiled, day after day, searching for that so-illusive, heavy-duty bullion.

Like I said, I looked it all up in the library. And what a tale I found. Here's some of the grit:

"One man's gold is his, two men's gold and you might as well tell the world," that was one of the sayings in 1865 – the year when the stampede hit the *Westlands*. Before then, there were

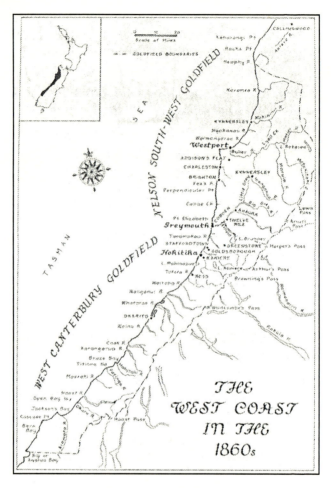

Some towns just 'disappeared overnight'

just 2,000 folk living around those parts. By the end of that year there were 15,000.

Nearly one-third of them were Aussies. Rough diamonds (if you'll pardon my mixed carats) up from the worked out claims of *New South Wales*. Some were Yankees, veterans of the *California* rush. Many were Kiwis, abandoning their *Otago* fields to the south in search of richer pickings. Others were Brits – English, Irish and Scots – newly-arrived adventurers who suddenly found themselves in a rainbow chase for the pot of gold. The word even reached *Canton*, and boatloads of Chinese turned up, too.

There weren't many women. In fact, finding one must have been almost as difficult as spotting some of the glittering stuff. Estimates put the ratio at about 5:1. The brave ones ran hotels and pubs; others went in for the servicing industry. "Ladies of relaxed virtue," as I saw them euphemistically called in one book.

For a while it was glorious mayhem. Towns literally sprang up overnight. *Hokitika*, south of *Greymouth*, became THE port/town for the treasure-seekers. Within months, the stampede had turned this bush-lined river and sandpit of a place into a bustling town of over 12,000 people. There were shops, banks, boarding houses, barbers, eating places, offices, warehouses...

Another overnight creation was *Okarito*. One account said that in no time it went from a deserted beach to an instant community with 1500 men, 25 hotels, 3 theatres, 2 banks, a harbourmaster, and enough grog shops to start a brewery.

What a rag-tag army the prospectors all looked! A brawny, tough living bunch of human termites who burrowed their way into the rock and dirt, then panned, sluiced and flumed the water through it hoping to rinse out a fortune.

Theirs were the names of legends. *Yankee Charley, Red Jack, Liverpool Dave, Black Sam, Gentleman George, Jimmy the Slogger...* and the ladies, too, like *Roaring Meg and Gentle Annie.*

The men wore the standard gold-diggers uniform: Bearded face, flannel open-neck shirt, moleskin trousers, leather boots and a "wideawake" hat. "At least a dozen languages could be heard in the bars or in the secret huddles where they discussed where the next strike would be," said one account I read.

They were a fidgety lot. Always ready with the get-up-and-go when a new rumour spooked them. Miss the word and miss the opportunity. Impatience is a virtue when you're in a Rush. "They are all mad by God," one shop-keeper is said to have cried as most of his town, lemming-like, disappeared into the bush.

Amazingly, in just three short years it was pretty well all over. More than half-a-million ounces of gold had been unearthed. Fortunes had been made and lost. Towns had come and gone. *Hokitika* was back to where it started. *Okarito* was down to a couple of diggers' huts. Some places just vanished off the map altogether. The rocks were all washed up, you might say. Down the

ONE WAY or ANOTHER

pan. *Tumble Weedsville*.

Quite a story huh? In America, you can bet your life there would still be fortunes being made from it. *Disneyworld* would be running the place, *Harrison Ford* would be starring in the movie, *Col Sanders* would be lickin' his fingers. But not in calm, conservative New Zealand where they still have petrol pump attendants, short-back-and-sides haircuts, and early closing shopping days.

Truth to tell, I had quite a job finding out much about it all, and historians lament the lack of documents. "It was all over so quickly no one seems to have had time to write down what happened," moaned one.

But all is not lost for us tourists. Never fear. We still have the Name Game to bring it all back.

Let's rejoin that drive down memory lane. From where I left off, here come some names which paint a darker story. *Graveyard Stream* and *Cemetery Creek* are problematic in the I-spy stakes. But what does it matter if this is the watery place where *McPherson* met his end? Or *Wilson*, or *Cannan*, or *Brady*? That's another 10 points for every tombstone, thanks a lot.

I wonder if they ever thought their names would live this long after them in black letters on a yellow board down this highway of their dreams? It's quite an epitaph.

And who on earth unearthed all their names anyway? I question. What a monumental task. It's a big responsibility, naming names. All that reading of old diaries, checking of ancient maps, listening to dusty folk songs... Maybe the government set up a special department. M'm, I wonder what they called it?

In this country, which is larger than mainland Britain but has less than 10 per cent of its population, I reckon that nearly everyone must be related to somebody or other on a signpost down the west coast.

And here's another turn-up for the I-spy contest.

The highway has twisted inland at *Haast*, leaving the sea at the apocryphal *Ship's Lookout*, and climbing up into the mountains towards *Mount Brewster* (another 10).

The names are taking on a different theme now. No points at all for the descriptive *High Bluffs*, nor for the ubiquitous *Imp Grotto*, *Thunder Creek* or *Fantail Falls*, and only a measly 1 for *Blue Pools*.

There's plenty of points for *Orman's Falls*, the *Bluffs* of Messrs

Douglas and *Clark*, and the *Flats of Cameron*. Although what those folk were doing up here goodness only knows.

Likewise, there's another couple of mysteries we can only guess at. Here's a sign that simply says: *Solitude No 2*. Sounds rather quaint, don't you think? But what do you suppose it means? And where is *Solitude No 1*?

Puzzle: Here's Solitude No 2 – But where's No 1?

Puzzle: Here's Half Bridge No 1 – but where's its twin?

And here's another puzzle. The sign says: *Half Bridge No 1* – but there's no sign of *Half Bridge No 2*. Better make it only half a point for that one then.

To be *Frank* ('tho I'm not as a matter of fact), the number of signs is getting down to more manageable proportions now that

ONE WAY or ANOTHER

*Queenstown,
with the 'Remarkables' mountains*

we are up in the mountains and we've left the goldfields behind.

Name Game over then. Notebook closed. And I am well on my way to *Queenstown* where there is snow and ice and a pal has told me there's the best ski-ing in New Zealand.

Just a sec. What did he say they called this sporting *Mecca*, I remind myself, pulling out the map from my luggage sack. "*The Remarkables,*" it says in big, bold letters. Now there's another name to conjure with!

Acknowledgements:

Stepping Back by Mark Pickering, Shoal Bay Press
West Coast Gold Rushes by Philip Ross May, Pegasus Press

© Richard Meredith and Mercury Books – all rights reserved

GOING FOR GOLD
Oi! Oi! Oi!

Sydney, Australia; September 25

THIS IS the story of how the gold medal for beach volleyball at the Sydney Olympics was won by a local TV actress and a DJ wearing red surfing shorts. It really was. Believe me. I was there.

The records will show differently. They will say that two super-fit, bronzed, bikini'd Australian girls named Kerri Pottharst and Natalie Cook beat two super-fit, bronzed, bikini'd Brazilians called Adriana Behar and Shelda Bede by two sets to nil in front of 10,000 people at a temporary stadium erected on Bondi Beach. But oh boy, there was a lot more to it than that.

Sporting *aficionados* awake screaming at night because beach volleyball is again (for the second time) accepted as an Olympic event. In terms of sporting purity they rate it alongside tiddly-winks and under-water basket weaving. But to TV producers and soap opera enthusiasts it is simply the best.

Forget all those sporting metaphors like quiet confidence, silent concentration, hushed support. Beach volleyball is big on entertainment value; and I mean BIG!

Bondi, and the 'sandcastle' volleyball stadium on the beach

ONE WAY or ANOTHER

Action!
The Aussie girls (far side) are all set

If you are into audience participation you'll love it. I'd describe the whatever-it-is as badminton played with hands instead of rackets, and a football instead of a shuttlecock. But the crowd's involvement... now that is something else.

So here we are in this sand castle of a stadium doing the Macarena between points, rocking with the Village People, swaying to the rhythm of the Brazilian drums, jumping up and down with the Mexican waves, and there's a guy out there helping us to do it just right.

Not an ordinary cheer-leader mind you. This is DJ/MC Dave and he's like no other Olympic official you have ever seen. Dressed in bright red surfer shorts, T-shirt, sunnies, and a white "spirit of Australia" hat, it's his job to make sure we all have a good time.

Somewhere down there on court there's an Olympic final going on. The coffee-brown Brazilian girls – hot favourites, 20 times champions of this and that, and as well-known in their

GOING FOR GOLD Oi! Oi! Oi!

country as Copacabana is to Barry Manilow – have raced into a sizeable lead in the first set.

But the Aussie girls are no possums. OK mate? Up on the terraces the party is getting into overdrive. Soon they've pulled up level and then – caramba! – they've stolen the point in a sudden-death decider to win the first set 12–11.

Let's have some fun, says DJ Dave, as the girls take a break. He takes us through a slow-mo of the Mexican wave to the sounds of Tchaikovsky's Swan Lake. It's hilarious. So who cares who wins or loses, life's a beach.

But isn't this the Olympics godammit? Isn't Australia only for winners... all that kind of thing? We are about to find out.

Dave comes off the neutrality fence in the middle of the second set. At 10 – 8, the Brazilian girls have again got themselves ahead and with sets usually going to the team that gets to 12 points first, things are looking tough for the Aussies.

They call a "time out", which means they need a breather. The girls have been out there for 70 minutes. Bending, stretching, twisting, turning, jumping, thumping. The sun is hot. Have they shot their bolt? Lose this set and the next one could soon be gone too. Game over. Nation in despair.

The crowd senses it's a defining moment. So does Dave. And he's got to do something PDQ (Pretty Darned Quick).

Lovely Deborah

Up above him there are 10,000 of us. Huge numbers of beach boys from Brazil are doing the samba. Even bigger numbers of Australians are doing the waltz with Matilda. The State Premier is in the VIP box. There's a row of models wearing not-very-much just where the TV camera comes zooming in.

DJ Dave spots Deborah Hutton in the seats at the front of the south stand. She's wearing a pink blouse. And she's looking lovely. Even me, a visiting Pom, recognizes her. Her picture is in the brochure they've been giving away to Sydney tourists. "Her face and name are synonymous with Australian style," it says.

The locals know her even better. She's what the commentators call a "TV personality" and just recently there's been a lot of her

ONE WAY or ANOTHER

A model audience for the TV cameras

in a classy ad campaign for the city's big department store. "Hey, look who we've got here," says a delighted Dave. Neutral? You must be kidding. "Our girls are in a bit of trouble out there. What can you do for us Deborah?"

Now that kind of intro could have been the kiss of death for lots of actresses I know. No script. No rehearsals. An audience of 10,000 hanging on your every word. Bit of a wobbler. But not for our Deborah. She's a pro.

There's been a chant around at these Olympics. It's somewhere between what they sing at rugby club booze-ups and the sound a cockatoo makes in the Outback. Deborah goes straight for it. "Let's hear it for Kerri and Nat... Aussie, Aussie, Aussie," she implores. "Oi! Oi! Oi!," comes back the throaty answer from Australia's Olympic Male Voice Choir. She goes again: "Aussie, Aussie, Aussie"... And so do they: "Oi! Oi! Oi!"

Oh boy, let's have a party tonight.

GOING FOR GOLD Oi! Oi! Oi!

*Medal
celebrations for the Aussie girls*

Out come the girls. And I swear that no one, really no one, could survive the combination that now hits the trembling Brazilians. DJ Dave has got the Backstreet Boys strutting their stuff. Half the nation is shouting Oi! Oi! Oi!. The modeling girls are up for the camera. Deborah the pretty one is leading with the High 5's. Like I say, it's party time.

The Aussie girls have a new heart. Rumour had it before today that they fell out with each other more than they fell in. But now they are playing like a perfect combination. Pottharst is the driving force. At 35, she's described as a veteran in the programme. But she's got the fastest service in the game. We know that because the clever IT thing on the giant TV screen up there tells us it just went at 85kph. Phew! Point taken. And the next, with a delicate drop shot from Cook.

Oh my goodness, the Aussies are equal at 10 points all. The party is turning into a rave. Pottharst hits another hammer service. The Brazilian nuts are cracking.

And now the end is here. There's a rat-a-tat-tat across the net involving all the girls. Ironically, Pottharst is already down on her knees in the sand when the ball goes past her nose – and out of court – for the final, definitive moment. They have not lost a single point since our Deborah came in with her Oi! Oi! Oi! Remarkable.

The Aussie girls roll in a heap of tears and cuddles down on the court. DJ Dave is trying to get the VIP box to join in with the hand-jiving-ohyeah. Deborah is posing for the camera; still looking very lovely.

Game, set and gold medal to Australia. Just like it says in the record book.

© Richard Meredith & Mercury Books – all rights reserved

Also see Appendix–2

TAKING THE PLUNGE

Cairns, Australia; September

IT'S 6.30am. We are on the company's bus. Bleery-eyed. Unshaven. Hung-over. "I hope you haven't had any breakfast," says the maniac with the microphone. "If you have, you'll be seeing it again soon." I knew then that it was going to be a tough day.

All the bravado in the pub last night had suddenly evaporated. Seen through the bottom of a glass, surrounded by macho Aussies, white water rafting is a doddle. No bother. Could do it in my sleep, mate.

The reality is very different. I'd rate it somewhere between the wide-eyed rush of high-roll gambling and the closed-eyed fear of death.

Rafting adventures with the Raging Thunder Company in north-west Australia start early. 6.30am is an obscene time for anyone to be considering whether they will still be alive by sundown. But that's how it goes on the trip from Cairns down to the Tulley river, one of the great white water venues in a continent that's has been blessed with more than its fair share of nature's challenges.

Roly, the grizzled microphone man, takes a macabre pleasure in setting out the rules for the day. No jewellery (male or female) – "we don't want you saving your gold necklaces when you should be saving yourselves," he says. And no sun cream lotion either – "we want to get hold of you, not a bar of soap, when we haul you out." Encouraging, huh?

He's directing his words at us – "rafting virgins" as he likes to call us – the brave ones who've put up their hands to say they haven't done it before. "Now I'm going to pass a form round for all of you to sign. There's a lot of small print, but basically it just says that if anything happens it will be *your* fault, not ours. OK?" We sign.

Amazingly, I find there are about 100 of us converging on this watery Big Dipper from here, there and everywhere. Interestingly,

ONE WAY or ANOTHER

nearly half of them are Japanese. But more of that later.

If you notice where I am, you'll know that Cairns is famous for its coral diving on the Great Barrier Reef. But when the weather's poor and the wind's blowing, there are those amongst us who can't do without an alternative adrenalin fix. That's why we are headed for the Tulley.

Let me just describe the scene. There are 18 rafts ('tho personally I would call them inflatable dinghies) made from some kind of toughened rubberized nylon stuff, which are about to set off on this assault course from hell. Inside each is an average of six thrill-seeking psychopaths who, for some reason best known to themselves, want to test their mettle against Fear Factor 10. Each has a man-who-knows in the bit at the back to shout the orders. We wear a crash hat, a lifejacket, swimming kit, a paddle, no sun cream and definitely no jewellery.

"Now, before we go, here's some instructions," says our Main Man.

"If I shout 'Go like hell' you paddle fast. Got it?" We got it.

"If I shout 'Get in left' you lot down that side throw yourself into the middle – and the other way round for you on the right. Got it?" We got it.

"And if I shout 'Hang on' then you just grab that rope down the side and don't let go. Got it?" We got it.

Easy peasy so far? Yes? Then why, I wondered, are we all trembling?

"Oh, and there's one more," continues the Main Man.

"When I call 'Group sex' we all jump up and down."

We what?

"Yes, yes. Sounds good eh? But I'll tell you more about that later. You'll see…"

So here we go, all 18 boats of us. Shooting the rapids, they call it. Fair dinkum, cobber.

Our Main Man introduces himself. "Just call me Fish," he says. A wiry, deep-tanned Aussie with flowing locks and shark-white teeth, he's been doing this River Tulley lark for 10 years; knows every current, every swirl. Maybe we should call him Eddy. I notice the other Main Men call him Boss. Why did we get him? I have a theory about that. It's to do with the fact that we have two lawyers on board. But I could be wrong.

Anyway, there are six of us. The two solicitors, two accountants,

TAKING THE PLUNGE

'Fish' (at the back) takes us down the Tulley

a marketing executive and me. Four blokes, two girls. They all come from fancy houses back home in Birmingham, I met them on this morning's bus. We have all signed the disclaimer, left behind our jewellery. But my guess is that it would still be a pretty expensive shipwreck.

We hit the first white water after no more than 50 meters. It should be called the 'Devil's Falls'. Why? Because it's simply evil. Nature has decided to place a series of granite boulders across the river here in such a way as to force the raging torrent into a gap in the middle. And that's where we must pass before plunging down into the swirling, foaming mass below. In the flash of thought that flits before the eyes in moments like these, I vision it as the mouth of a neanderthal giant sucking in drink through extremely bad teeth. Evil, like I say.

"Go like hell," says Fish. "But, but..." I am trying to shout a

ONE WAY or ANOTHER

warning only the words won't come out. The gap between the rocks, you see, is clearly not as wide as the boat. But what can you do? The Birmingham mob are already going for it. Paddling like demented dervishes. No Professional Ethics to hold them back. Nothing in their Terms of Reference. They're just intoxicated with the thrill of life.

At the very, very last moment I hear the words from Fish: "Get in left" and we hurl ourselves – the three of us on that side – into the belly of the boat. Result? Up goes the left side, being immediately so much lighter than the right, and we squeeze through the gap like one of those Evil Kinevil tricks where he flips the car up off a ramp onto two wheels. We are through in a instant, although if I'd had my breakfast it would still be following me.

I hear the next command somewhere in mid-air. "Hang on," says Fish.

Now that's the one you don't argue with. Don't even think about it. Just dive back onto the side and hang onto the safety rope with all your might. No worries, huh? Yeah, and I'll be a wombat's uncle.

Anyway, call it what you will... fate, luck, judgement. Whatever. But by the time we hit the water once more the boat is, miraculously, back on an even keel. Don't think it's over yet though. Oh no. For now comes the plunge downwards into the base of the waterfall over which we are currently flying. Smack goes the front end, juddering into the *maelstrom*. Smack, smack, smack, smack go our safety helmets, headbutting those in front. Smack go our teeth, clattering together in collective shock. But somehow we come up alive. Wet. Very wet. But still alive.

Needless to say, not everyone is as fortunate as us. Because of the safety rules, we wait a little bit downstream while the other boats come through. Or, let us say, try to come through. I counted half a dozen which come to grief in one way or another... startled adventurers suddenly catapulted into space, now popping up like so many corks above the angry surface, ready to be hauled in by us and the others. One boat, full of Japanese, flips over completely as they make a horlicks of the midflight manoeuvre. Nips in the air, I am tempted to say.

And this is only the first white water test. There are dozens more over the 10km stretch. Rapids, plunges, squeezes, teases. You name them, we get them. Thank you God for Fish and all his experience. A twist of his master paddle here, a shout of his sharp commands there, and we live to tell this story to people like you. He knows every rock, every hard place. "It's my office," he says.

We get to know the language of disaster, too. There's a "wrap" for when the boat runs aground on a rock, there's a "big rinse" for when a boat gets into an uncontrollable spin and, worst-case scenario, there's the "thunderhit" for when a boat turns completely upside down. Come to think of it, maybe they should re-name that one: "Doing a Japanese."

Then there's the falls themselves. Each one gets a name. A colourful lot – and no room for sexual modesty either. "Wet and Moisty" speaks for itself really. And the one which precedes it is, naturally enough, called "Foreplay."

Further on, "Double D" has a story to go with it. Seems that a rather ample tourist girl got sucked into the whirlpool that sits at the foot of this particularly nasty rapid. And yes, you've guessed it, the water pressure had ripped off both her lifejacket and bikini top by the time rescue arrived. That one's gone down in folklore with the Main Men.

All of which kind of brings me back to Group Sex, as promised...

It happened just when all in our boat were thinking, rather smugly, that Fish was invincible. "It's a wrap," he says as our boat climbs up a rock and – for the first and only time – fails to slide off again onto its next intended direction. "Group sex," shouts our hero.

Now this is exciting! Surely? We all get off our backsides and – under Fish's exhortations – jump up and down in unison like we were on a bouncy castle at the fair. Result? A multi-orgasm. Or something like that, as the boat frees itself from impending disaster and we all flop back, relieved and exhausted, to rejoin our battle with the swirling torrent.

The Japanese are a barmy lot. Ever wondered why they go in for those spiders-down-the-trousers contests on TV? Well now I know. Just to watch them at white water rafting is to understand their national psyche. They are all quite mad. Instead of being afraid to die, like the rest of us, they actually seem to want to. Never again will I wonder what drove their pilots to go "kami kazi" in the war. Nor less why they fall on their swords when things don't go well. Needless to say their tip-up rate far exceeded every other nation's.

Five hours it took to get down the Tulley rapids. Five hours of bend and stretch, of splish and splosh, of fear and terror. Only one person has ever actually died while in the company's charge, Fish told us over a beer later. Caught his feet between the rocks and the water pressure kept him under for just too long. "It was one of those things; just unlucky that's all; nothing anyone could have done. Another fellow did the same thing not long after but we got him out. It's fate you see. When your time's up..."

I ask Fish how it rated, our course today. "Level 4," he said. "The official definition is: 'moderately technical rapids with continuous need to manoeuvre.'" Then he added, with a chuckle: "Wait 'til you get to Level 6 – the book says: 'extremely difficult rapids. Necessary to be in control but very rarely possible.'"

Anyone for kami kazi?

© Richard Meredith and Mercury Books – all rights reserved

THROWING FRIZBEES AT THE MOON

Broome, Western Australia; September

STRANGE things happen after you've spent a week in the bush in Australia. Take my word for it. You can finish up throwing frizbees at the moon.

The place is a patch of wasteland in the middle of nowhere. Well, about 20km out of Port Hedland going up the coast of Western Australia, if you really want to be precise. But 'wasteland' and 'nowhere' will do to be honest. Because that's what Australia is – it's full of nowhereness.

For people like us, from Europe, the place is just enormous. And there's hardly anyone about. It's approximately the size of North America but you could fit the whole of its population into New York. Get the picture? Most of it is, well, just empty.

How come, I ask myself, that in this place of no bodies they have so many Somebodies? People like Kerry Packer and Rupert Murdoch, Clive James and Dame Edna, Olivia Newton-John and INXS, Ned Kelly and Crocodile Dundee, Alice Springs and Flying Doctors, champions of the world in rugby and cricket, and a tuckerbag full of Olympic winners? It is really quite amazing. If there is a Lord above, he must have sprinkled some very concentrated stardust round here.

Anyway, back in the bush, when it's time to kip down for the night and the place is empty, then anywhere will do. We simply turn down an unmade track off a highway which goes presumably to somewhere a long way away.

The big 4-wheel Toyota landcruiser rumbles over the stones, just like it has every day, and most of the nights, for the last week. There are five of us on board, intrepid travellers on an adventure safari into the wilderness of this Wonderland of Oz, led by Phil, our been-there-done-that guide/driver, who's our leader, inspirator, educator and changer of music tapes.

"This will do," he declares as a clearing of hard, flat earth miraculously appears out of nowhere.

We unload the wagon for the umpteenth time. Tarpaulin on

ONE WAY or ANOTHER

The big 4x4 will rumble over anything

the ground, sleeping bags inside their dark brown swags like insect cocoons. Our beds for the night. Our last night under the stars in never-never land. Now for the table, the cooking pots, the plates, the cutlery and the kettle called Billy... all the stuff you need for an adventurous lot who want to throw away their westernized comforts for a week and live like natives in the Outback of Australia. Paid good money for it, too.

It is, by now, a ritual. Each of us knows what to do. No need to ask. It's a team. We ARE natives godammit. And tonight is the last night.

Soon the meal is over. Now what to do? It's nearly midnight. The moon is oh-so-bright, casting an eerie semi-light across the starry emptiness. Someone gets the frizbee out. I mean, what else could you possibly be expected to do when there are five of you, all cultured, civilized people feeling like natives in the middle of the night in the wilderness of Western Australia? Of course it's frizbee time. No worries, cobber.

The first problem soon arrives. A wayward throw somewhere off into the darkness is retrieved by Carolyn, lately a carefree wood nymph from the Land of Billabonga and formerly a 26-year-old nurse from Edinburgh, who reveals with a strange exclamation to the assorted players, that she's found a railway line up there over the ridge. Really? A railway line in the middle of nowhere? And us about to kip down beside it too? "Oh well, what's a railway line doing here?" we say. Or something like that. "So what?" It's that kind of a night.

Then there's a more substantial threat. We have heard already the sound of the dingos, those wolf-like howlers in the woods up yonder. But been-there-done-that-Phil has told us they are harmless. And we believe him. So that's OK then. No, it's the roar from the nearby bushes that really sorts out the girls from the boys. Unmistakable. It is the noise made by an extremely large bull in the Outback of Western Australia when he finds that his sleep is unexpectedly disturbed by the antics of several beer-crazed frizbee throwers in the middle of the night. Believe me, you only need to hear it once and you think you are shortly going to die.

Amazingly, Phil, the fountain of all things, still remains unfazed. Even when his flashlight picks out the huge frame of the rogue bull thrashing about, dazzled, in the undergrowth, he says not to worry.

"He'll be more scared of us than we are of him," he says with a reassuring confidence. M'm...

"The thing is, he won't be used to so many people, Toyota wagons, campfires, all that kind of stuff. It's him that's frightened."

The rogue bull: 'More scared of us'

ONE WAY or ANOTHER

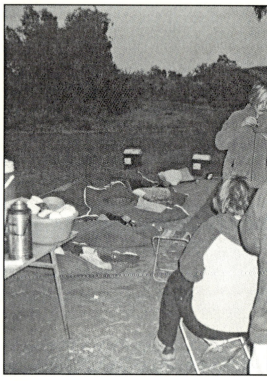

Sleeping in a row to 'face the enemy'

Oh yeah...

"Well look, if you're still worried, I'll sleep at the end (of our open-air dormitory) and I'll drive the wagon round to block him off. He'll stay well away, I assure you."

We settle down for an uneasy night cocooned in our swag bags: Carolyn, her friend Aileen, also a nurse; Dani, an aerobics teacher from Switzerland; Phil, the brave one; and me. The frizbee is near to hand. It's just the kind of weapon we natives need for frightening off rampaging bulls in the middle of the night.

The first goods train rumbles past barely half-an-hour after we have gone to sleep. Phil tells us in the morning. We didn't even hear it. The bull is nowhere to be seen; must have wandered off in search of frizbee throwers somewhere else. Not even the friendly dingos have put in an appearance. So Phil was right after all.

Worried? What, us natives? You must be joking mate!

There were, in fact, six of us when this whole escapade started a week or so ago in Perth. It was raining then, and cold. That was one of the reasons why a safari into the warmer weather up north, up into the bush and along the coast to Broome, seemed like a good idea. The other was the thrill of exploring where few of us have gone before. The kind of adventure-theme park you won't come across in Seven Sisters Road. Or Sauchihall Street for that matter.

The sixth member of our bush-whacking gang is Jane. A real Aussie in her own right. Fourth generation and proud of it. Up from South Australia, she is a teacher who's had-it-up-to-here with the pressures and needs a break. Shame for her, she has to bail out after five days when duty calls her back to her other life – a 100-acre farm which she bought as an antidote to her stressful job. She didn't want to leave us. It made her cry.

It is quite a gang, us would-be natives, who set out to spend a week with each other roaming through the wilderness of the Australian Outback. Mornings, noons and nights. Character-building. Bonding. Team-working. All the kind of things you read about in those "Art of Good Management" handbooks.

Phil, the leader, is 32, single, and a real-life Mr Body Beautiful. He's built himself into a hunk through a regime of weight-training and exercise that would make an international athlete weep, and he keeps it that way with a constant stream of ecologically correct potions and pills that he produces from a cavernous black holdall beside him on the driver's seat. By character, he's a shy man. But as a specialist on all things Australian, ancient and modern, he's an absolute whiz; forever pulling facts and figures from his filing cabinet of a brain to keep us interested.

Jane, the stress deserter, is soon swooning over him hotter than a kangaroo with sunstroke. The combination of her farming knowledge of flora and fauna is a perfect foil to Phil's facts and figures, and the pair of them bamboozle us with a never-ending stream of commentary. Being 40, divorced, and not often in the company of shy Adonises, she is frequently overcome by a kind of strange neurosis most often found in a quivering jelly. But not to worry cobber, it keeps us all amused.

Our route is up the coast to rugged Geraldton, and then to Monkey Mia, where the wild dolphins perform. Next comes Carnarvon, with the English-sounding name, and Coral Bay

ONE WAY or ANOTHER

where the sea is so clear you can see the coral and its fish world almost from the beach. Inland now to Tom Price's town, the iron-ore man who taught this country how to pay its way, then through Karijini park to Newman in the wilderness, and on to Port Hedland where the nightime frizbee championship is held. Stunning!

The towns are only blips along the way. Something to aim at. You soon learn that about this barren land. We would call them "rural communities" back home. There's really no one there. Just a roadhouse (gas station), a pub, a clutch of shops and a shower if you're lucky.

They are also, sad to relate, the places where the Aboriginal outcasts hang out. You see them in little groups, lolling about, drunk mostly; once-proud men of ebony black skin and white Brillo-pad hair now relegated, with their saggy-clothed women, to the fringes of life. The government, afraid of a blot on the landscape, has given many of them back their lands and told them to go home. But everyone knows they are being squeezed to death between the Rock of tradition and the Hard Place of progress.

Between the towns is our safari land – the wilderness where the spiniflex grass grows amongst the eucalyptus (gum) and the melaleucas (paper bark) trees, and the wildlife lives. The place is teeming with it – red kangaroos, rock wallabies, numbats, dingos. We even see, rare apparently, the rat/cat-like northern quoll. Then there's the birds – wedge-tailed eagles, kites, magpies, ungainly emus, the loud-mouthed cockatoos. Yes, it's all here, and more, for those who'll go a-waltzing Matilda with me.

And this is where we build our campfires at night, this is where we sleep under the stars. "You may not know this," says Phil, pulling down the microphone in his cab like some kind of frustrated airline captain, "but the bush park we are now travelling through is about the size of Belgium." Cor!

"Oh look at that," says an exultant Jane, not to be outdone. "People have survived for days out here by drinking the juice from Sturt's Desert Peas" (spectacular blood-red flowers we have just passed on the trackside). Like I say, this tit-for-tat info is just what you need when you are an apprentice native on an intensive training course.

All through the first few days while we are visiting strange lunar landscape rock formations known as the Pinnacles,

Day 1: Hot start in the park at Pinnacle Rocks

deserted beaches at Lucky Bay where the sand is white as snow, clambering down hidden gorges in the Kalbarri national park, and communing with those dolphins at the inappropriately-named Monkey Mia, poor Jane wears the hang-dog expression of a labrador who wants to play, but can't persuade her master to throw the ball.

Finally, after a day of snorkel-diving to see the rainbow-coloured fish at wonderful Coral Bay, she tries the alcohol trick to haul down Phil's defences. It's her last night with us natives. The hotel bar we've found provides the atmosphere, the day's warm sunset makes the perfect stage. But then, oh woops, suddenly the heavens open and there's a mad dash to cover up with hats and waterproof clothes and plastic things. Dampened ardour. Game over. Isn't life a bitch?

The nurses from Scotland, as you might expect in a job where they have seen it all before, and more, take everything in their stride. Carolyn, a spinal injuries specialist from Edinburgh, clucks about like the ward sister she wants to be, organising things here, supervising there; all the while issuing timely warnings about the danger of snakebites, food poisoning, breaking legs and other such minor irritations.

ONE WAY or ANOTHER

Aileen, her pal of seven years, another 'aged-20-something' nurse, this time from Glasgow, giggles through it all – peering out myopically through little porthole specs perched on the end of her nose, puckering up her cheeks in a permanently chubby grin. Such is the nature of things, she probably finds all of this adventure lark more difficult to cope with than the rest of us. But she does the best she can, and we love you for it, possum.

In fact, of course, it's turning out to be just the kind of textbook experiment in human relations which we thought it would be. A bunch of people thrown together, not exactly on a desert island, but on a deserted island continent certainly. Will they/won't they get on? Will there/won't there be fallings out? Who'll emerge as leaders/followers? Who'll keep the spirits up/pull them down? Who'll pair up, or not, with whom? Let's put them under the microscope. Let's see what happens to this batch...

But the answer is: We all get on like long-lost chums. Seven days and more of mornings, noons and nights and there are no fights. No quarrels. No coupling ups. No fallings out. Just lots of fun, hard work, helping each other out, and all the rest...

Maybe Dani has the hardest task. 25, a policeman's daughter from Lucerne. Used to discipline, yet with a fiercely independent mind. But my God she's Swiss. A foreigner! Aussies, Scots, English – how can she possibly cope with the dialects of a language which we often have trouble understanding ourselves?

Answer: She gives it her very best shot – and more; never once backing away from trying to find the words which for her are so difficult; polishing up on her schoolgirl English, until, with each passing day, she masters it some more. Once, in complete exasperation, she decides to shock us all by learning as many swear words as she can. "What a bloody, fucking, shitty, piddle," she exclaims as she spills the morning coffee. After that, she can do no wrong.

Anyway, the days come and go. Days when our happy band trundles through the wasteland in the big Toyota truck without seeing another living soul. Nights with our bush camps and wood fires. Washing in streams, swimming in rock pools, sleeping under the stars, cooking our food, washing the dishes. Keeping our dignity, keeping our humour. More than 3,000 long kilometers through the Australian bush on an experience of a lifetime.

THROWING FRIZBEES AT THE MOON

And now, at last, the journey is ending. Here is Broome, the final destination; the flower across the other side of the Great Sandy Desert; the tourist town where there are hot showers and cold beers, and supermarket shelves and food served to you on plates, and internet machines, and shops to develop your photos... We rumble into the place with the windows open, singing our hearts out to that pop-rock classic "hooked high on a feeling". It seems the perfect choice. Even the sun takes its cue - sinking down, red and glorious, below the horizon on Cable Beach just as we drive into the car park.

Now where's that frizbee, someone asks. Let's give it one last throw.

Journey's end:
Sunset on the beach at Broome

© Richard Meredith and Mercury Books – all rights reserved

THINGS THAT GO BUMP IN THE NIGHT

Chumporn, Thailand; August

I ONLY saw it when I got into bed. Horrible. Awful. Right there above me. Defying gravity. Stuck to the ceiling like Spiderman; only this wasn't Spiderman – or even a spider. It was a dragon, or a lizard, or a gecko, or an iguana... something like that. And it was huge; I mean HUGE.

Just the other day, in a cage at the reptile zoo, I'd seen another whatever-it-was. But I couldn't remember which. Anyway, no time for wondering now – no time for switching out the light like I was going to do. This monster thing was stuck there on the ceiling, a foot long or more, legs and arms (or are they all legs?) splayed out, its ancient armour-plated body looking horribly heavy high up there above me.

Any second now; any second... I could just visualize it free-falling right down onto the bed beside me. Or, far worse, thudding plum into my face with a direct hit before I could move.

But I did move. You bet I did. I was off that bed in an instant. But what to do next? Now that's the question.

I was alone in the guest room at a friend's country house in Thailand. Most people can't afford one house in Thailand, let alone two. But he can. He's a top man in his profession. Grade 10, the ultimate. Honoured by the king for services to the country – all that kind of stuff. His place out in the sticks is what we would call a farmhouse back home; a big old timbered place tucked away in the forest, 100 meters or so down an unmade track off the nearest road. He'd invited me there to meet his family.

We'd both slept in the guest room the night before; it was so big. But now he'd gone back to the city and I was left there to sleep my last night alone.

I guess it was around 10 o'clock. Inside the main house the women had all gone to bed. There were generations of them – the grandmother of 86, daughters in law, sisters in law, aunts, cousins. Loads of them. Like I say, it was a big house. They'd spent all weekend cooking and fussing about. But now the men

ly, the very thought sends
ONE WAY or ANOTHER

were all gone. All except me. And the ladies were in bed.

So what shall I do now, with this monster dragon/lizard thing on the ceiling? Do they bite? Do they sting? Do they breathe fire down their nostrils? Oh God, why can't I remember what it said in that guidebook at the zoo?

I decide to take a chance. Not to be brave, you understand. Just to take a chance. There's no way I can sleep in this room. Not with that gecko or whatever-it-is poised to plop down onto me at any moment. I mean, can you imagine...? Ugh, the very thought sends me into horror movie land.

OK then. Stay calm. Consider the options. Can't sit up all night watching it; that would be ridiculous. Can't lock it in here and go outside to sleep; that would be absurd. No, I'll just have to catch it. That's what I'll do. But what on earth with?

A quick recce of the place leaves me little choice. It's a big guest house all right. But it's sparsely furnished. A fishing net? You must be joking!

In the end, to be absolutely honest, the only objects I could find that were even remotely suitable, were a child's plastic potty (left thoughtfully for me by the old granny in case I needed to pee in the night) and the top of an enormous earthenware urn, shaped like an upturned dish, and which I can grasp by its ornamental spike of a topknot.

The idea being, you see, that I would knock the THING off its perch, catch it like a cricket ball in the potty, and then ram the German-helmet lid down on top before it could spring out again. Easypeesy. Hey presto. Good as done. I'll carry it outside in triumph; let the fine little chap zip off into the woods. Back to nature. Free again. Quite unharmed. Got the picture? Me. Bit of a hero, really.

Trouble was, the THING wouldn't play ball. Up there on the ceiling (it must have been 12-foot high) his 180-degree, all-seeing eyes were watching my every move as I circled down below him. No way could I reach him. Not even standing on the bed. And anyway, can you imagine the kind of contortions it would have taken with potty poised in one hand while the other knocked him off with my upturned lid thing? And supposing he missed the potty? What then? Splodge – right on my head. Imagine! No thank you.

So I resorted to one of the lesser-known abilities of amateur gecko hunters. It's called cushion throwing.

Now the idea of this game is that you gather up all of the cushions you can find in a rarely-used guest house deep in the forests of Thailand (plus any spare pillows that just happen to be close at hand) and you make a big pile of your ammunition in the middle of the room. Then you proceed to take aim at the gecko. Not to hit it, you understand. In fact, just to miss it; but close enough for it to realize that it ought to move.

Next stage – and here is where only the very best skills succeed – you make it steadily work its way downwards to a height at which catching it neatly between a child's plastic potty and an upturned dish thing with a spike on top becomes a distinct, and physical, possibility.

Well either that, or by cunningly opening the door and driving the THING in that general direction, to hope that it will spot the obvious opportunity and slope off into the night. Not such a triumph, it must be said. But something of a moral victory nonetheless.

Anyway, there I am, feeling rather pleased with myself, standing on the bed and adopting the afore-mentioned style of small-game hunting which you will certainly not find in any textbook at the local library, raining cushions towards – but not quite at – the target, when one of the old ladies, alerted by the noise, appears at the doorway.

Why am I pleased? Well because I have managed to get the THING down, after a series of expertly-aimed cushion deliveries, to (a) the kind of height where I am considering giving it serious potty training, and (b) where if it whiffs in an unexpected breath of sweet night air I figure it might just realize for itself that a dignified exit from this unusual bombardment, is on the cards.

But the old lady is certainly not amused. In fact, quite the opposite. My command of the Thai language, and hers of English, being equally non-existent, mattered not a jot. She summed up the scene in an instant. I had gone stark-raving mad.

It didn't help that the object of my cushion-throwing was out of her sight. But the look on her face, as she surveyed the picture in the dead of night, of me standing on the bed, potty in hand, ammunition piled up all around, chucking 'bombs' in the general direction from which she had so recently appeared, and grinning like a Cheshire cat, left her in not the slightest doubt: I had taken complete leave of my senses.

How do I know? Well it was easy to tell by the way she ran screeching into the main house and the speed with which the

ONE WAY OR ANOTHER

four big bolts were sent thundering shut across the back door.

But alas, worse was to follow because, horror of horrors, a quick glance over at the wall confirmed that my cunning enemy had himself taken advantage of the screeching diversion, and simply disappeared. I mean, yes, gone. Skidaddled. Up'd sticks. Vanished. But where to? Oh God, he certainly hadn't taken the fresh air option; the old lady had seen to that. So where?

Gingerly, I searched every nook and every cranny. It's a big guest house. As big as a double garage back home. I looked under the chairs, under the bed, on top of the wardrobe. You name it, and I peeked into it, or over it, or round it. But no gecko. I felt almost lonely. In a strange way I'd got kind of used to him being around.

And then it dawned on me. Up there in the ceiling; all 12-foot high of it, there were recesses and beams and things, which not even me with my new-found agility, could investigate. Somewhere up there, he'd either gone out the way he'd come in, or maybe he was just sitting there waiting – waiting for me to get back into bed, waiting to take up position again, waiting for lights out, waiting to take his revenge...

And that's when I remembered the mosquito net.

It had taken up precious space in my big back-pack from the very beginning, but I had only begun to begrudge it recently. Spray cans and ointments had dealt with the few mosquitoes I'd found in India and Nepal, and here in Thailand, and I confess that I'd marked it out mentally as the first thing to go when I did my very next load-lightening audit. But it was now that I discovered why I'd brought it – it wasn't to deter mosquitoes after all; it was as the ultimate protection from night-flying geckos. Perfect. I settled down on a settee, as far from the bed as I could possibly get, cocooned in the damn thing. And do you know what? It works.

I woke myself up every couple of hours, as you do in these kind of circumstances. But there was no gecko in sight. Not one.

An uneventful night, I wouldn't call it. But a night without attack from above, certainly. All I can think is that those bulging eyes somewhere up there must have stared down in disbelief at the oh-so strange creature wrapped up in a tight, white, shroud of muslin, and decided, after all, to leave well alone.

Come to think of it, perhaps it reckoned I was a chrysalis which might hatch into some kind of gecko-eating monster in the morning.

© Richard Meredith and Mercury Books – all rights reserved

JEWEL IN A TARNISHED CROWN

Bali, Indonesia; August 29

LATER this week the trial is due to begin of ex-President Haji Mohammad Suharto of Indonesia on corruption charges which allege that he swindled his country out of $US billions through fake charities.

On TV, the 79-year-old former ruler looks a broken man. Sick; twitching in the camera lights; a shadow of his old self. But when the judges find him guilty – as surely they must – millions will rejoice.

The people of Asia – his part of Asia – believe that Suharto has blood on his hands, and a deceit in his soul, which the world should never forgive.

There's a Chinese saying for people like him. It goes like this: "If you eat stolen food, be sure to wipe off the evidence from around your mouth."

But autocratic Suharto never did that. Such was his arrogance of power that he left the evidence there – and he brazened it out for years. The people, his people, saw the dirt around his mouth. But he thought he was untouchable.

A taxi driver in Singapore saw the dirt. One day he picked up a Chinese businessman returning from Indonesia. The man told him how, around 30 years before, he had been running a small grocery store near the barracks where Suharto was the major in charge. "He came to me with a proposition that if I could supply the place with socks he would fix the contract and he and I would share the profit. There were many thousands of socks to be supplied. We did the deal," he told me.

Suharto was on his way. Corruption. The dirt around his mouth.

Not long afterwards, the world was to see another, more evil face. In a bloody coup when many people died including several of Suharto's fellow generals, he seized power as the ultimate leader of Indonesia – that strategically important archipelago of islands in the Indian Ocean which contains the world's fourth

ONE WAY or ANOTHER

most populous nation.

Five years later, bolstered by a secret agreement under the pretext of cleansing a communist threat, the Americans and Australians stood quietly by as Suharto ordered his troops to invade neighboring East Timor (then a Portuguese colony).

What followed was more than two decades of some of the worst butchery the world has ever known – and Suharto brazened it out again. In 24 years of occupation, Indonesian troops tortured, maimed and killed an estimated 200,000 Timorese men, women and children in an appalling outpouring of barbarism while the super powers played dumb because it suited their "political strategy".

In the end, thanks to the bravery of Timorese resistance fighters and the ceaseless campaigning of journalists like the Australian John Pilger to tell the world what was going on, the UN at last stepped in and put sufficient pressure on Suharto to force him out of office.

Right now, in an act of wholesale appeasement, peace-keepers from the global community are helping the Timorese to restore their shattered country. Elections are to be held in a year's time and the nation will again be free and independent.

But what of Suharto, the man with dirt on his face? In typical style he's cocking his familiar snook at the world. First, he's already organized himself an official pardon, no matter what the verdict of the court in his corruption trial. Second, he's placed his family in high places right across the spectrum of Indonesian industry, keeping the channels clear for them to continue siphoning a fortune – already estimated at $300 billion – out of the country. Third, he's made sure that his old military commanders are able to pull the strings of current ruler Abdurrahman "Gus" Wahid, a man who seems to share the same disdain for his people.

When asked why his lady vice-President had failed to show up for an important meeting recently, he dismissed the questioning by saying she had gone home to take a bath. "It's typical of the Suharto regime – they have all convinced themselves they are on a different planet to the rest of us," a senior official told me, but only on the promise of anonymity.

But for me, the worst of Suharto's crimes is not his alleged corruption, or even his regime of terror in the annexation of

JEWEL IN A TARNISHED CROWN

Timor. It is how he has abandoned his own people. Left them high and dry.

Indonesia is potentially a rich country. Blessed with nature's raw materials like minerals, rubber and oil, it is a necklace of islands that spills its jewels across the ocean between South-east Asia and Australia. Towards the southern end is the brightest gem of all – the so-called "island idyll" of Bali.

Here, the world's tourists are invited to spend their nice hard currencies enjoying some of the most wonderful beaches and scenery to be found anywhere in the world. The people are warm and friendly. They want to help their country. They want to help themselves. But they don't know how. They have been given little or no financial guidance, planning or direction – and it shows. An estimated 60% of the men folk are out of work and the local economy is in chaos.

Here's my own little story to illustrate what is happening ...

IT'S 12 o'clock. High season. Yet we are the first customers of the day. The little girl in the gold and silver shop has that wide-eyed innocence which is the very hallmark of Bali. She greets us at the door like longlost cousins. How are you today? You're very welcome." She giggles it out with a sunshine smile. And so we go in – while the taxi driver slopes off to claim his "commission"... a cup of cold tea for bringing us here.

Inside, the place is like a Bond Street store. Row upon row of glass-topped display cases, all with glittering collections of gold and silver trinkets. Here the rings, here the bracelets, the necklaces, the earrings, the brooches, the knick-knacks. Most of them made on the premises by skilled craftsmen sweating over their soldering irons, heads bent low over the piece they are melding into something for lady followers of fashion.

Trouble is, there are loads of places like this. It's the third one we've been to within the last half-mile. There are lots more in this street. In fact, there are scores of them in this little town. And the next. And the next. Get the picture? It's what the economists would call over-capacity. Same story, too, for the other staple store lines – wood-carving and clothes-making. Everyone knows the name of the game: It's called 'Let's relieve the tourists of their cash!' But no one has told them the rules.

ONE WAY or ANOTHER

You can't fault anyone for all this enterprise in paradise. Everyone is certainly busy, busy, busy making things. But there just aren't enough punters to buy even half of what's on offer – even if they wanted to. Result: (a) the stores are piled higher and higher with stock that will never move; and (b) the pricing structure is shot to shreds. The lesson is: You just can't beat those old economic maxims of Supply and Demand. But the outcome is so sad it's laughable.

We quickly find an intricate silver trinket that takes the eye. In an instant, the happy brown-skinned girl has laid it on the counter. Then another, and another. It doesn't take a genius to make out what's happening. She only has to see your eyes alight on something for more than a second, and it's out from the display and onto the counter to the accompaniment of her babbling chatter of "me give you good discount. You buy. Please you buy..."

In short, she's desperate to sell something. Anything. It's pitifully obvious.

Soon there are dozens of pieces of shiny jewellery littering the counters and our bubbly salesgirl has been joined by a gaggle of others, all badgering us to part with our money. It's like bees round the hibiscus. Talk about the customer being king...

Anyway, now comes the so-sad-it's-laughable bit, because for those of us from the West used to fixed prices in the High Street – let alone Bond Street – the delicate art of negotiating swiftly comes into play. Ah, did I say delicate? Well let's change that to brutal. And as for negotiating, let's call that a one-way track to the bargain basement which even a kindergarten tycoon could follow.

The conversation, if that's the right word, goes something like this:

Salesgirl: "The price on the ticket is US $60."
Customer: "Why is it in dollars?"
Salesgirl: "Because we like dollars more than our own money"
(M'm, that says a lot in itself eh?). Now the next part:
Salesgirl: (completely unprompted) – "We put the price on the ticket, but we don't really mean it." Oh ? "Yes, we give you discount of 30% straight away." Oh?
"Then you say a price below that, and we can fix something in

the middle. Yes?"
Customer: "Well no. I'm afraid not. Why don't you just tell me the lowest price you will accept and we'll start from there?"
Salesgirl: "But we don't have a lowest price. You just tell me what you will pay. Yes?"
Customer: (as a joke): "Oh well, US $20 then?"
Salesgirl: "M'm. Good. Yes. That will do."
Customer: "Ah, just a moment. That was my first price. Now we negotiate something lower. Yes?"
Salesgirl: (hesitating): "Oh dear. I get manager OK?"
Manager: "How much will you offer then?"
Customer: "Oh I don't know... maybe US $10?"
Manager: "M'm. I just get boss" (on the 'phone).

There then follows a muffled conversation somewhere in the background between the manager and his boss on a mobile phone. Soon, back comes the manager wearing a broad smile: "It's your lucky day. My boss says OK. Right?"

Negotiations over. A hallmarked silver trinket worth US $60 of anybody's money for just US $10. Can't be bad. Candy from a baby eh? But so-sad.

Far too many shops in Bali are selling too few things for too little money. They are on a fast-track to economic suicide and every tourist knows it. Although, of course, they would never say so.

The island folk have been left to founder by Suharto and his cronies. Without financial guidance, lacking education and with little or no commercial *nous*, they are yet more victims of his arrogance of power.

Dirt, blood, deceit and disillusion – that is the legacy of his evil regime.

Postscript:

1. This story was submitted to the *Daily Express*. It was well thought of, and they considered some of it might be used later depending on future developments.
2. On September 28, Indonesia's supreme court rules that Suharto is too ill to face trial. His lawyers say he has suffered three strokes, is mentally unfit and clinically depressed. The prosecution appeals.

3. In October, Suharto's youngest son Hutomo "Tommy" Mandala Putra is sentenced to 18 months jail for his part in a $ US 10m land deal scam. He later goes on the run.

4. In December, the Indonesian provinces of Irian Jaya (West Papua) and Aceh campaign for self-rule and legislators call for the impeachment of "Gus" Wahid.

5. By April, secessionist groups throughout the archipelago are campaigning for independence, Wahid has now been censured twice by parliament, the military admits it is no longer in full control and Indonesia's economy is in the doldrums.

Further reading:

Distant Voices by John Pilger, Vintage Books (Random House).

© Richard Meredith and Mercury Books – all rights reserved

EAST GOES WEST FOR 'NEW AGE' WOMEN

Delhi, India; June

THE WAYS of the West are reaching out to women in India, tugging off their apron strings as one of the world's last great bastions of male "supremacy" starts to crumble.

For centuries, India's women – the vast majority of them (80%) followers of the strict Hindu faith – have had to cover up in public and draw a veil over fashion by wrapping themselves up in voluminous saris.

Custom has it that they walk discreetly behind their menfolk in the street, arranged marriages are still very much the norm, and work is usually confined to manual or menial labour.

But the ways of the West's "New Age" woman – and Man for

Ancient and modern: A mother and daughter in Mumbai

ONE WAY or ANOTHER

Doing the dishes at the village tap

that matter – are sweeping in like the monsoon rains.

After China, India has the world's biggest population, and you don't turn the habits of a billion people on their head in a hurry. But the pace of change is quickening.

Out in the country – and most of the sub continent is extremely rural – women are as likely to be seen as men labouring on building sites, working in the rice fields, or carrying the produce to market. And all that's on top of washing the clothes in the local stream or cleaning the dishes under the village tap.

But it's in the big cities that you can see the changes happening first. In Mumbai (the new name for Bombay) it's the "20-somethings" who are strolling now in their designer jeans and hugging boyfriends in the street on their way to the vibrant disco scene.

In Delhi, India's capital city, smart worksuits are replacing the sari for girls-about-town who are holding down career jobs now in finance, sales and marketing. And in Kolkata (was Calcutta), where an amazing 300,000 students study at the university, young people are picking up the pace of new trends in fashion in a big way.

EAST GOES WEST FOR 'NEW AGE' WOMEN

What's helped to push things along is a unique triple breakthrough in the beauty stakes with Diana Hayden, then Miss India, winning the Miss World contest in 1997, Yukta Mukhi, a model from Mumbai, holding the current Miss World title, and Lara Dutta, the 23-year-old daughter of a retired Indian Air Force Officer from Bangalore, winning the Miss Universe crown earlier this year. They have proved to everyone that Indian girls can look the biz in a swimsuit – something Hindus have rarely been allowed to see before.

In this land of stark contrasts and contradictions, abject poverty rubs alongside prosperity. 62% of women are classed as illiterate (33% of men) and vast slums and shanty towns sprawl alongside high-rise suburbia in the cities. Average annual income is well below £500 per head and the poorest are in the countryside where tribalism is still rife and it's not uncommon for an adulterous wife to be stoned to death by other women in the village. Divorce is virtually unknown.

But Westernism is starting to take a big hold on things. It's piping into nearly every home through more than 20 TV channels –

Same old story: Washing out the smalls

ONE WAY or ANOTHER

many of them in English – serving up familiar images of glittering lifestyles, dance and music. The internet, too, is having a massive influence, and the Indians are seeing more and more of us and our culture at first hand.

Richards Branson's Virgin Atlantic has linked up with Air India in a joint venture to promote more passenger traffic between London and Delhi, while the charter airlines are already doing a roaring trade bringing planeloads of fun-seekers – especially from Britain – to Goa on the west coast for a holiday season which begins in October.

All-night raves and beach parties which last a whole week over Christmas are becoming as legendary for Goa as they have been for Ibiza in Spain. And although the locals don't like it much, they do like the money it brings in.

Politics too are changing. 50 years after the British pulled out and gave India her independence, the domination of the Congress Party has been broken and the current BJP national government is filtering more democracy into the country's own gentle brand of communism. The British influence is still all around however, with English as the official second language and cricket and hockey the major national sports.

Even the first steps to privatisation are being proposed, with airlines and ports scheduled as the first to go, 20 years after Mrs Thatcher broke away from State-control conventions in the UK.

In such a vast country, where every region has different cultures, languages and dialects, and where people physically look and dress differently, change is bound to come at different speeds. Heart-throb film divas, who could have the choice of hunky leading men, still bow to their parents' wishes of an "arranged" partner.

But Westernism is still breaking out in the cities come what may. In Delhi, as in Mumbai, the queues are longest at the counters in McDonald's, while signs for Wimpy, TGI Fridays and Pizza Hut are just around the corner.

Veenu Sandhu, a 27-year-old journalist from Delhi, summed up the new mood. "There's absolutely no doubt that things are changing," she said. "We are not throwing out our traditions completely. In fact, most young women have two wardrobes now – one for saris and one for Western dress. We are bombarded by what the West is doing fashionwise through TV and newspapers and we want to be part of that. After all, wearing jeans and a T-shirt is a

EAST GOES WEST FOR 'NEW AGE' WOMEN

Veenu: Typical of India's new young women

lot more comfortable!"

Coping with Westernism is throwing up questions throughout Indian society and bringing about a thorough examination of values.

Critics point out that the use of drugs, especially in heavily urbanised areas, is an increasingly significant problem. There has been a sharp rise in rape and sex-related crime, and the censorship laws are being tested much more often in the courts.

"Many of us are worried that liberalism could bring about big changes in our family lives," a young father working as a travel consultant in Mumbai, told me. "We have seen the explosion in divorce, separation and single-parent families in the West, and there are fears that it could lead the same way here eventually."

ONE WAY or ANOTHER

Look out! There's a heavy load ahead for this lady worker, while (below) women turn their hands to road building in Delhi and doing the washing in a local stream near Trivandram

Footnote:
This story was submitted to the *India Express*.

AND THE SURVEY SAYS ...

Mumbai (Bombay), India; June

FOR a long time now, it has been a contention of mine that we are being swamped with surveys. I am sure you've noticed it, too. Every day in newspapers and magazines, or on the radio and TV, some organization or other is busy telling us the result of their latest survey, or vote, or poll, or sample, or whatever.

Mostly I ignore them. In fact, such is my perversity, I actually like to hope that large numbers of those being asked will deliberately mislead the questioner with false information. And, as a result, they will publish and be damned, so to speak.

It has happened once or twice, quite famously I believe. And I am glad of it.

Anyway, to come to the point, despite my better judgment I read another of those surveys recently. It purported to be a league table of "The Most Corrupt Countries in the World" – and India was right up there with the best (or worst) of them.

I consulted my Indian friends about it. Was it really so? I asked.

Answer: true/sometimes true/not true at all/a downright lie?

And, as a supplementary: If true, what occupation is the most corrupt? (excl. Politician, which is taken as read, and therefore has no "new information" value at all).

Answer: tick the box, only one please...

Being faithful to my cause, and just in case they have pulled the same misleading trick on me, I shall certainly not tell you their answers even if, overwhelmingly, they opted for "sometimes true" and "railwaymen". But I can tell you about some things which happened to me on the Indian railways only a couple of days ago. Then you can make up your own minds.

Central Station in Mumbai is a perfect example of the chaos and confusion which exists in that frenetic, over-populated city.

It begins half-a-mile away with streets clogged by cars and taxis on their way to unload passengers. It continues as you get nearer, with people on foot, struggling along with bags and baggages, barging their way through the throng of sidewalk vendors. And it

ONE WAY
or
ANOTHER

Chaotic scenes on the station platform

ends with a *melee* of bodies in the booking office and on the platform.

To make it worse, I am in a hurry. I have had news that my daughter Clare, who is on a teaching project a long way further south somewhere, has a bad eye infection. And I want to find her.

Gurcharan Singh, my taxi-driver of the last half-day, has taken the problem to heart. He has children of his own; he understands my concern.

I am in his slipstream as the tall, turbaned Punjabi strides out ahead, picking his way through the knots of people, many of them women with young children, just lying or sitting about on the booking hall floor.

Where to buy the ticket? So many counters, so many people, so much confusion. My guidebook tells me there are meant to be some privileges for foreign visitors. Gurcharan spots his target and takes aim: "Tourists queue here," it says. There are, maybe, 100 people already in the line and none of them looks like a tourist. "No, not that one," I countermand, "let's try here."

We change course towards the window sign which says: "Military – current and old soldiers." Oh well, it's worth a try. I am dressed in T-shirt, jeans and a baseball cap with the insignia of a well-known sportswear company on the front. I am not currently in the army and neither, heaven forbid, am I an old soldier. But there is no queue. And I am in a hurry.

Gurcharan towers beside me. "I need a ticket for this afternoon's express to Kanniyak...," it's a long word and I cannot get my tongue round it. But the ticket man already knows what I mean. He cuts me short. "No chance you get on today," he says. "All reservations must be made at least four hours before departure. The seating plan is all done. You come back again tomorrow. Yes?"

Oh Hell, I hadn't thought of that. It must be like an airplane. I would need a sleeper-car bed for two nights and an air-conditioned carriage. Things like that would all have to be planned out and allocated on some master plan like it was a jumbo jet. And there is now barely an hour left before take-off. Too late. Damn!

We start to walk away. Gurcharan has a sorrowful frown above his bearded face. My head is down. What a disaster – another 24 hours to wait; another day lost in my expedition to find Clare.

But then, of course, I had forgotten about that special way in which things can get done around here. My survey allergy, remember?

Within seconds, a small, laughing man with a mop of black curly hair, is at my shoulder. He has overheard my predicament. "You want to go today?" he says. "I work for railways. I can fix it. You come with me. Yes?"

We get to a corridor with a door at the end of it saying "Staff only".

"You give me 2,700 rupees now. In cash. OK?"

It's 600 more than my ticket would have cost. But, more to the point, I wonder whether we will ever see him again at all if I hand it over. I take Gurcharan's arm, turn him aside, and whisper: "Well, what do you think? Can we trust him?"

Gurcharan, tall Punjabi

"Yes," he says, "but just in case, I will also tell him that I will come and find him afterwards if he doesn't come back." I watch curly mop's eyes roll as Gurcharan jabbers out his threat, see the twitch on his lips as the big man draws a line across his throat with his finger. M'm, looks like he's got the message. I count out the money. Now we are marching in haste to another part of the station; the laughing man, the Punjabi and me – puffing and sweating at the back with my bags.

Suddenly, our leader ducks into an office doorway and tells us

ONE WAY or ANOTHER

Home of the Debating Society!

both: "You just wait here. OK?" Does he really think we wouldn't?

It doesn't take long. Curly-mop is back with a smile on his face and a piece of paper in his hand. It's handwritten. But it's official – got the proper stamp on it, too. I have my ticket.

Gurcharan checks it over for me. Yes, right train; yes, right time; yes, sleeping car; yes, air conditioning... His eyes are laughing. I am booked on the Kanniyakumari Express! Who says surveys don't get it right?

Postscript:

It happens later on the same train journey. Kanniyakumari is the Land's End of India, the southern-most tip. It takes 48 long hours to get there from Mumbai.

It is the morning of the second day. So far, other than my ticketing shenanigans, there has been nothing else remotely in the category of corrupt, illegal or untoward. In fact, if we were on a ship, I would call it plain sailing.

Anyway, at this point, we have drawn up at some out-of-the-way station in a place whose name I cannot even remember, where there are many like me from our train who are stretching our legs with a stroll along the platform.

AND THE SURVEY SAYS...

*Full speed ahead
for the Kanniyakumari Express*

I didn't see them coming. But then, I suppose that is as it should be. The local police chief has come up to me from behind and, in no time, two or three of his officers have got me surrounded.

"Are you wearing perfume?" the boss demands, aggressively. I can hardly stop myself for bursting into spontaneous guffaws. I have been in the train compartment for many hours. The odour factor on my personal hygiene-o-graph would not impress. But perfume? Oh no.

"Sure? Are you sure?" he questions my denial. And then, I swear, he comes close enough to actually sniff me. "Yes, well I can't say I can smell it," he continues, reassuringly, as he gathers his men and marches them off in the general direction of the station master's office.

Now strange and unexplained as this was, I perhaps would not have thought too much more about it – except for what happened after another stop, a few miles further on, when a business-like Indian came bustling along our carriage offering cheap perfume to anyone who will make him a sensible offer.

I notice, too, that he is dressed in the uniform of a ticket collector.

© Richard Meredith and Mercury Books – all rights reserved

Also see Appendix–3

LIFE IN THE FAST LANE

Cairo, Egypt; May 28

IT SEEMS good to be back in Cairo. The place has at once a big city buzz about it, an amazing, sprawling mass of humanity where skyscrapers and corkscrew-topped mosques jut up alongside mud-walled shanty towns and downtown poverty.

I have been down on the train to Aswan, to see the great dam, and back along the Nile by boat to visit Tut's tomb in the Valley of the Kings. And now I've flown in from Luxor to Cairo's chaotic airport.

I feel that buzz again as we drive into town in the shimmering heat of midday. Come to think of it, the higgledy-piggledy road system and the way these people drive, says everything about them.

The roads are like a tangled ball of wool, patted about by a playful kitten. A mixture of highways, and freeways and byways all knotted together. It's an all-action game to try and follow along your strand of wool without being thrown off course by the pinball antics of the cars rushing all around.

Then there's the trial of anticipation – by which I mean spotting your turning up ahead and getting yourself in place in time to take it before you are washed away helplessly in the swirling, motorized current.

All that, plus the initiative test of dealing with an unexpected donkeycart that suddenly appears trotting along in the slow lane, or avoiding the cyclist with a death-wish who needs to get across four lanes of Formula Fiats because he has just spied a friend sitting on the sidewalk.

Mind you, I say lanes of traffic without conviction – because, although there are white line markings on the road, no one takes any notice of them. It is quite possible, for example, to get three cars abreast in a two-lane highway. Or even five across three. In Cairo, it is. Believe me.

No rules either for which side to overtake (or, if there are any, they are just ignored). Drivers whiz by on this side or that of the

ONE WAY or ANOTHER

car in front, darting through the smallest gap as soon as one appears, and merely toot-tooting a sound of warning, often when it's far too late to take evasive action anyway.

Everyone seems to have got themselves into this habit and they go around with one hand permanently hovering just above the hooter button. Wherever you are, and at any time of day or night, the air in Cairo is constantly punctuated by the sound of car horns toot-tooting above the roaring flow of traffic.

All big cities have their taxi populations. I will later be buzzed by the swarm of black and yellow wasps in Bombay, and left gasping by the scooterized tuk-tuks of Bangkok, but you can be sure there is no taxi driving anywhere in the world like there is in crazy Cairo.

Maybe they do it just to keep foreigners from driving or hiring cars of their own. Everyone races around like there's no tomorrow. But taxis are the worst, and there must be 100,000 of them in the city.

It's not at all difficult to get a driving licence (although I am told the regulations have been tightened up a little recently) and, judging by the number of times my own drivers have failed to find the asked-for destination, neither is there any kind of "local knowledge" test like there should be.

Taxi driving is, of course, on the face of it, an easy way to earn a living in a place where there are not a lot of easy livings to be earned. Consequently, this city is overwhelmed by a flying army of black and white ants for hire. There are grossly too many of them and simply not enough trade to go round.

Competition is so fierce that you find yourself often approached on the street by a taxi driver who has abandoned his vehicle to tout for business on foot. Either that, or he has stopped off to pass the time nattering with his mates, and so, as you pass, you are often startled by a voice, hailing you from the distance somewhere, asking: "Hey my friend, you want taxi?"

I once asked a driver how business had been that day. "You are my first customer," he admitted with a grin. It was 8 o'clock at night and he reckoned he had been "working" for 12 hours. My fare was a generous £2. A job collecting camel droppings at the pyramids would pay better, I conclude.

Not surprisingly, because they spend so much time with their owners, taxis in Cairo often look more like mini mobile-homes;

LIFE IN THE FAST LANE

*Collecting camel droppings
would pay more*

being decorated garishly with artificial flowers and knick-knacks of every description hanging from whatever lends itself as a hook – mirrors, knobs, handles, sun visors.

Several I've been in have shown a nice line in tufted carpeting

ONE WAY or ANOTHER

on the driver's dashboard. An elaborately-ornate box of tissues is a standard fixture and, somewhere handy, there is usually a picture of the wife and kids to talk about with passengers.

On one journey, I was even offered a cup of tea. It happened this way: When the driver turned and asked me: "You like tea?" I must admit I took it to mean, you know, either: "Did I want to stop somewhere for a cup?" Or, because I was so obviously English, simply: "Did I enjoy drinking tea?" That being the opening gambit for some kind of discussion.

Imagine my amazement, then, when he produced an ancient type of kettle contraption from one of the glove compartments, plugged it into the cigarette lighter, and proceeded to boil me a cup of tea. He poured it out too, as we weaved in and out of the traffic, and handed it over at a junction. "I can't believe you just did that," I blurted out.

The vast majority of Cairo's cars have bumps and dents from a thousand scrapes and journeys. Many of them are miraculously patched together – although my guess is that hardly any would pass a proper test of roadworthiness.

Most of the taxis seem to be Fiats, presumably because of their price and economy, although I did hail a Mercedes one day that was 25 years old and painted dark brown, an odd colour for a taxi, but, as the driver explained, he had used a cheap tin of camouflage paint left behind by the British army in World War II.

The police, who are everywhere, seem to turn a benevolent eye on all of it. Speeding, driving without proper care and attention, driving without lights, failing to stop at traffic signals – they ignore them all like it was only natural.

On the other hand, maybe that's the only way. After all, around here, if you arrested one driver for a traffic violation, you could finish up arresting half the nation.

© Richard Meredith and Mercury Books – all rights reserved

APPENDIX

THESE WE HAVE LOVED...
Recommended places to stay or visit

1. Streets

London: Oxford Street...
   for giggling Japanese tourists, if nothing else.
Paris: Champs Elysee...
   wide-open spaces and the Arc de Triumph.
Hong Kong: Nathan Road, Kowloon...
   changes, like a chameleon, by day and night.
Singapore: Orchard Road...
   clinging on to former grandeur.
Bangkok: Kosan Road...
   street vendors, back-packers and rickshaws.
Sydney: George Street...
   Australia's answer to Sunset Boulevard.
Auckland: Queen Street...
   like going down a ski-jump to the harbour.
Buenos Aires: Avenue de 9 Julio...
   spectacular 16 lanes (widest in the world?).
Los Angeles: Sunset Boulevard...
   America's answer to George Street, Sydney.
Zurich: Bahnhofstreet...
   high-class walkthrough from station to lake.
Washington: Pennsylvania Avenue...
   prime (p)residential neighbourhood.
New York: Times Square...
   neon-lit centre of hustle, bustle and hype.

For all-round interest – 'tho not for shopping – visit **St. Charles Avenue, New Orleans**. Travelling the long, oak-lined street is like journeying through a time tunnel. One end, downtown, leads to the 200-year-old French Quarter, always colourful, sometimes wicked and ancestral home of Dixieland jazz. Then come back through the Garden District past 19th century *Gone With The Wind* plantation mansions with manicured lawns, and finish uptown at the city's vibrant and modern university. You can go the whole distance, round circuit if you like, on an ancient streetcar for a bargain $1.50. The "cars" have been working the avenue since 1835.

2. Hotels

(max. cost £30 a night, negotiated or otherwise, and often a lot less)

New Delhi: Center Point hotel...
        central, safe and surprisingly comfortable.
Kathmandu, Nepal: Ambassador hotel...
        modern oasis on the hippie trail.
Hong Kong: Pearl Seaview hotel...
        calm among the storm and a cosy bar.
Bangkok: Thai hotel...
        well-placed, live music, personable.
Singapore: Beach hotel...
        handy for most things, 'tho not the beach.
Sanur, Bali: Peneeda View hotel...
        lumbung in the garden; seaside idyll.
Cairns (Aus.): Travelers Oasis hostel...
        everything a back-packer could wish for.
Christchurch (NZ.): Camelot hotel...
        classy and central.
Wellington (NZ.): Trekkers...
        cheap, but very cheerful.
San Francisco: Adelaide Inn...
        European pension in theatre district.
Weedon (Northants, Eng.): Globe Inn...
        traditional, English country pub/hotel.
Christchurch, Barbados: Nook apptms...
        guesthouse with pool and cricket chats.
Tallahassee (Flo.): Collegiate Village Inn...
        bargain.
Washington: Bullmoose B&B...
        brilliant position, amazing breakfasts.
Montreal: Hotel du Manoir St.Denis...
        nicely laid-back; heart of Latin Quarter.
Vancouver: Burrard Motor Lodge...
        clean, reasonable price, central.

BANGED UP TO DATE

There's a new use for old prisons – turn them into hotels. The Hotel Lowengraben in Lucerne, Switzerland, served as the region's jail from 1862 until just a couple of years ago when the authorities sold it off and opened a modern alternative nearby. The new owners have maintained the theme. Bedrooms are the original cells with barred windows, bunk beds and security combination door locks. There's even an old guillotine on the top floor. Some serious offenders were held here including – in more recent times – the "parking lot killer" and the "bedroom murderer."

In Ottawa, Canada, what was the Carleton County jail from 1860 – 1972 is now an international hostel for back-packers. The nation's last public hanging (of Patrick Whelan for assassinating a politician) was held here in 1868 and the noose they used is still on display. Cells were just 6ft wide by 9ft deep although no one actually has to sleep in them now, thanks to a conversion which has turned the place into a 150-bed hostel of dormitories, private and family rooms.

Carleton jail – now a hostel

3. Boats and watery bits

Egypt: Lazing down the Nile on a cruise boat from Aswan (where the dam is) to Luxor (Valley of Kings/Queens).

Australia: Ferry from Sydney harbour to Manly, out past the bridge and opera house. White-water rafting on the River Tulley at Cairns in Queensland. Flatboat in the wetlands at Kakadu park, Darwin.

Dubai: "Penny ferry" across the city river to market.

Hong Kong: Ferry across the busy harbour to main island.

New Zealand: Three-hour crossing from Picton (South Isl.) to Wellington for just £7. Ferry from Auckland Harbour to Devonport also great value at just £2 return. Eerie silence and penguins in Milford Sound.

Caribbean: One-man ferry to Pigeon Island from Rodney Bay, St Lucia. Deep-sea fishing for tuna and marlin in the waters off Barbados.

Lucerne, Switzerland: Round the magical lake with its mountain views.

USA: Private trip from Fisherman's Wharf around San Francisco Bay, Alcatraz and under the bridge(s).

Statten Island ferry (free) past the Statue of Liberty in New York Harbour.

Brilliant Cruise Line trip all round Manhatten Island seeing some of the world's most famous buildings from their reverse sides.

Canada: Ferry from Tsawwassen, Vancouver threading through the islands to Swartz Bay in Victoria.

APPENDIX – 1
Newspaper Stories

See: Gunfight in Paradise

This was the original *'background feature'* story, filed from Fiji to the *Daily Express* in London, just hours before the army mutiny began.

THE PRICE OF POLITICS IN PARADISE
Vitu Levu, Fiji; November 2

THE QUEEN'S face is still on the banknotes, but the currency is close to going broke in paradise.

Images on TV screens and newspapers around the world of George SPEIGHT and a rag-tag band of supporters attempting to stage a coup in May in the South Pacific paradise of Fiji have faded from the memory. But the grass-skirted, floral-shirted islanders have been left to pick up a bill of around £100m as a result of what happened – and they are struggling to survive.

The Speight gang struck on May 19, taking over Fiji's parliament building and other key installations, and holding the prime minister and most of his cabinet hostage in an attempt to grab power. Within days, it became obvious that he didn't have sufficient support from the military to carry through the coup.

But although he quickly lost the plot – quite literally – it was 56 days before all the hostages were released and Speight gave himself up. Two soldiers had died and a journalist was wounded.

Today, Speight's motives are still unclear. Fiji's community is spread over 300 islands and rumours abound. The pragmatic theory is that the coup was a racially-inspired attempt by the indiginous Fijians who feel their homes and livelihoods are threatened by the fast-increasing number of immigrants from India.

It's an intractable problem because the influx has been going on for generations and there are now almost as many Indians or Indo-Fijians among the islands' 750,000 population as native Fijians.

Other theories suggest that Speight, a businessman known to

ONE WAY or ANOTHER

have been in financial trouble and equally well-known for his persuasive eloquence, hatched the plot to smokescreen his own difficulties; or that he was simply the front-man in a big-business syndicate which abandoned him when it became evident that the army would not give the coup wholehearted backing.

Whatever. Since his arrest he has continued to be held on a prison island while the authorities amass evidence to back their charge of treason and the few soldiers who supported him face courts martial.

Speight's "show trial" will presumably reveal the truth – but that is not now expected to happen until next year. Meanwhile, paradise is counting up the cost of those days of drama, or "madness" as one community leader put it to me, and trying to restore some kind of normality.

Tourism – which is Fiji's biggest earner – has suffered most. Before the failed coup, numbers were at record levels. Around 400,000 visitors came to the islands last year, spending an estimated £180m. Nearly half of them were from Australia or New Zealand and 30,000 of them British. The UK was the fastest-growing sector with more than 5,000 tourists (a record) arriving in February alone.

But all that changed when the wheels came off in May. Numbers in June, July and August fell by two-thirds and estimates from the Fiji Visitors Bureau suggest a loss in tourist revenues over last year of £56m. Add to that the £4m chipped into a promotion fighting fund by the islands' tourist industry, matched by their travel trade partners worldwide, plus the discounts and special deals now doing the rounds, and the cost jumps by another £20m.

Life in the paradise islands is still far from normal. Soldiers continue to man roadblocks around important sites and a night-time curfew is in operation. The sugar-cane harvest, badly delayed by the disruption, will be late with a prospective loss of product worth £8m, while other contracts throughout the Fiji economy have been cancelled and hundreds of workers laid-off.

It pushes the total cost to over £100m so far. ILISAPECI MATATOLU, marketing services manager from the FVB, lamented, with her head in her hands: "Years and years of work have gone to waste through these moments of madness by Speight and his rascals." She continued: "It's been a huge blow.

APPENDIX – 1 THE PRICE OF POLITICS IN PARADISE

And although everyone is determined to rebuild from the damage, our fear is that it could so quickly happen again."

Whether Speight's intention was to touch the raw nerve of racialism or not, there is no doubt that tension between the islands' communities is great.

30 years after their independence from Britain, the native Fijians fear that their farms and businesses are being taken over by the more ambitious and commercially-astute Indians. They have reacted by driving thousands of them out of their homes and forcing them to abandon their jobs and savings.

The tension previously erupted in 1987 with another coup, led by army officer SITIVENI RABUKA, which led to a change of government and a re-writing of the constitution. This time, a number of interim government appointments have been made and "free" elections have been promised in 18 months time after which demands for a further revision of the constitution will be considered.

Last weekend, when the Indian community would normally celebrate the annual DWALI holiday with fire-crackers, gifts and street celebrations, all was quiet in the capital of Suva. Shops were shut and people stayed at home.

Island newspapers have stories daily about suspects from the coup – mostly army personnel – being brought in for questioning, and a commission has been set up to invite information from the public. The authorities remain jittery. Last week three journalists on the local radio station were interrogated after a critical piece on an interim minister and emergency legislation forcing the media to reveal its sources is threatened.

But it is the cost to the economy that is likely to do the most damage. The price is rising daily and to make matters worse it is the loss of tourists' hard currency which is hurting most in Fiji where the currency is already 17% down against the US$ this year.

The annual summit of South Pacific countries has just broken up with no announcements about neighbour aid – but senior financial observers are suggesting that something has got to happen to underpin the economy – and quickly. Before the attempted coup, Fiji's treasury reserves were said to be around £270m and what's happened will have knocked a huge hole in that.

ONE WAY or ANOTHER

It will not be easy for the electorates in Australia and New Zealand to swallow loan offers to their troubled neighbours while their own currencies and economies are faltering, and the IMF will probably insist on an acceptable outcome to the election and constitutional issues before considering support.

Britain and the Commonwealth, because of their historic ties, look a possible saviour. But with a rash of indigenous racial issues now breaking out, not just in Fiji, but also in the Solomon Islands, Tonga and Samoa, they may be worried about the stability of the whole South Pacific.

Over the last decade, the region has been swinging away from its old allies and building relationships with Asia on trade, finance and cultural issues, and the focus may therefore turn to new "friends" like Japan, to provide a solution to Fiji's cash problems.

Meanwhile, those who have invested in the coral and coconut paradise, continue to try and surf through the difficulties. "What can we do except press on and try to protect our businesses?" said brothers Adrian and Robert Wade who run the Hideaway at Sigatoka, one of the best-known hotels on Vitu Levu, Fiji's main island.

Originally from Australia, the brothers have built up their hotel complex over 15 years only to see occupancy levels crash since the coup. "We are starting to see daylight again – and we could be full again next month," said Robert, former chairman of the Australia-Fiji Hoteliers Association, "but we are having to work exceptionally hard at marketing and discount deals.

"But we are among the lucky ones – it will take some businesses years to get back to where they were, and others will never recover."

Whatever happens, there has already been a heavy price to pay for politics in paradise.

© Richard Meredith and Mercury Books – all rights reserved

APPENDIX – 2
Newspaper Stories

See: Going for Gold Oi! Oi! Oi!

One of the biggest success stories of the Sydney Olympics was not on the field or track, but on TV. *The Dream*, a late-night show hosted by *Roy and HG* alias John Doyle and Greig Pickhaver took a sideways look at each day's events with typical Australian larrikin style. It became such compulsory viewing over the Olympic fortnight that an audience of more than 2.5m watched the final show – "an unheard of figure for a late-night Australian programme," according to the entertainment press. This story, filed to the *Melbourne Age*, uncovered a different angle to the tale:

SYDNEY OLYMPICS
Sydney; September 27

IF THEY struck gold medals for commercial winners at these Olympic Games, Tim Warner would be up there on the podium right now.

Tim Warner – who's he? Answer: He's a relatively humble exec producer with *Channel 7* in Sydney who's bright idea is going to earn them A$ millions.

It's not what you know – it's who, goes the old saying. And Tim is pals with the hottest two properties in town: Roy and HG, hosts of *The Dream*, Ch 7's nightly alternative look at the Games, whose following is racing up to cult proportions.

Tim knew the duo from their old days on radio, through their time on *ABC*, and put up the idea of them doing their thing to Harold Anderson, Ch 7's Head of Sport. It could be the most lucrative team selection he's ever made.

Everyone is talking about their larrikin show... a tongue-in-cheek version of the day's events with memorable take-offs of the weightlifters, gymnasts and synchronised swimmers amongst many other things. Tennis icon Billie-Jean King is among their latest fans. Here as coach to the American tennis team, she's on record as saying they should come back with her for TV over there.

ONE WAY or ANOTHER

But the boys will be staying put – and earning *Ch 7* mega bucks in the battle to pull in advertising revenues after the Games have finished.

TV earns most of its money from ads and sponsorship – and how much it gets depends critically on audience numbers. Right now, *Channel 7's* viewing figures are off the charts because of the Olympics. But their real game is to keep those new viewers from deserting back to *Channels 9* or *10* when the sport is all over.

The money at stake is huge. *Ch 7's* director of sales and marketing Maureen Plavsic reckons the TV ad spend has already expanded by maybe A$100 million – of which her Channel has won the majority. Keep their viewing numbers up and there will be more fortunes to come.

Not surprisingly, Roy and HG have already been signed up for further shows, *Ch 7's* corporate marketing boss Deborah Quin told me today. So too, have golden-boy Ian Thorpe and wonder-girl Cathy Freeman. There are also big serials being plugged like *Treasure Island* and *City Central*.

Quin refused to release details of *Ch 7's* revenue gains during the Olympics but when figures for the Quarter ending this month are released, expect them to be startling. Next Quarter, on the back of the big O and leading up to Christmas, promises to be better still.

And if they retain anything like the numbers of viewers from the other channels that they hope to – thanks to Roy, HG and others – then next year's ad contracts, starting January, will make *Ch 7* a fortune.

Step up Tim Warner. If they haven't given you a medal yet at *Ch 7*, at least it must be worth one helluva pay rise.

© Richard Meredith and Mercury Books – all rights reserved

APPENDIX – 3
Newspaper Stories

See: And The Survey Says...

My two-day train ride in India from Mumbai to Kanniyakumari was (at the time) the longest single train journey I had ever undertaken. This is a much abridged version of the "View from a Visitor" story which I filed to the *Indian Express:*

TRAIN RIDE IN INDIA
India; June

GURCHARAN, the tall Punjabi taxi-driver, sits with me in the carriage for the half-hour before we leave. Already he's become a friend, a trusted soldier looking after his charge, refusing to leave until he's sure there are no more problems.

My first companion comes in – a middle-aged woman who owns a commercial art business in Mumbai and who is going to see her daughter down in Conchin. Then there is Paul, a younger man who actually works for the railways and is on a free-for-staff ride.

The last place – there are four seats which turn into bunk beds at night – is not taken when we leave, and various people come and go on it during the journey.

So these are the people I will spend the next 48 hours with, on a journey of 1,000 miles, zigzagging across six provinces and down half of India. They, about 700 others I should guess, and me – the only westerner on the train.

It soon becomes clear what kind of train it is. An express – yes, but not of the non-stop variety. We pull up at about one station in every three. After the big diesel engine comes a baggage car, then three carriages for those who can't afford a sleeper but can afford a seat and basic comforts, four carriages like ours, each sleeping about 60, and then another eight, without doors or windows, where the poorer travelers lay claim to any space they can.

We click-clack our way out of Mumbai. The city seems to go on forever. Those in our carriage – who I have already nicknamed The Debating Society – reckon there are 17 million people living

ONE WAY or ANOTHER

here, but it's obvious that no one can be really sure.

What an extraordinary place this is. Outside our windows, we peer at a kaleidoscope of ancient and modern, rich and poor; one moment a suburb of high-rise offices and luxury apartments, the next, areas of terrible deprivation and the pole and plastic-sheeted shanty towns of MAHARASHTRA which tumble down almost to the track.

From inside our comfortable compartment, it seems like their lives are helter-skeltering by, although the fact is, it is their world, not ours, which is standing still.

Each station presents a similar picture; crowded platforms bursting with hubbub. There are vendors and hawkers shouting out their wares, wheeling their carts up and down beside the carriages; railway guards, signalmen, platform keepers and station masters; the *hoi polloi* who just sit around, numb from hunger, or lie asleep on benches. And beggars, too. They come to our carriage – little girls with grimy faces, a cheeky grin, and no food in their bellies.

Inside the train, we privileged few are getting the vendor treatment from red-coated boys who trot up and back to the pantry carriage with trays of samosas, or potato pancakes, or snacks of nuts and crunchy mixtures, sweetmeats, water ice-creams and, naturally enough, Indian tea – hot, sweet and milky.

The Debating Society is hard at work. Shastri, the business lady, is complaining that too many clever Indians are taking their talents overseas. "Do you know," she protests, "one-third of all the programmers at Microsoft are Indian?" Now that's a good one to get us going.

Outside, the scenery is beginning to change as we go into KARNATAKA province. Not so many slums as we approach each stop, I notice. And the dress is changing, too. Here now are the white Nehru-style upturned-boat caps of a different region.

It is a pattern which I begin to look forward to as the journey progresses. Every region has a different culture, different dress, different dialect. India's fascinating contrasts are beginning to unfold. The countryside is changing, too. No more now the urban sprawl. Instead, green fields, pastures, trees and hillsides. Warm rain, also, as the misty skies unload.

Inside our compartment it is time for supper. A curry of this, or a curry of that? My new-found friends tease that it will be too

APPENDIX – 3 TRAIN RIDE IN INDIA

spicy for me. Soon, the whole carriage smells like the corner takeaway.

The Debating Society is meeting again. Paul, the railwayman, who usually works at Head Office, reckons that fares should be subsidized by the State so that people can always get around. He is supported by a railway engineer who has just joined the train. It's a fair point. "We make our money out of freight," he says.

Next morning, the panorama is different again. Now the stops are much less frequent. The landscape is more arid (and it stays that way all day), the population is more thinly spread.

Small villages scatter round the track from time to time; the houses always basic – single-storey, flat-roofed. Now they have red tiles, now thatch, but always there's a shrine to the gods in amongst them somewhere.

On the station platforms there are fewer vendors but more produce. Sacks of beans, bags of tea and flour, packages of fancy goods – not for our train, but the next freighter that comes along. It's far more rural. I notice chickens strutting outside one waiting room, and a pig roaming loose at another.

Begging is ever-present. It seems like they give the worst cases in each village the "honour" of begging from us, the better off people on our train. Nearly every stop features a badly-deformed man or woman in some distress and there are always dirty-faced children claiming orphan status or worse.

The British set up the Indian railway network and there are still reminders everywhere. Even the platform announcements are in English and some of the station names could be straight out of the Hornby annual: Katumani Halt, Guntakal Junction, Ernakulam Town, Trivandram Central.

In mid-afternoon there's a longer stop. We are nearly halfway. The engine needs changing from diesel to electric for the overhead cables. The people here in ANDHRA PRADESH have darker skins and I have seen a few palm trees along the way. It's noticeably hotter.

Ah, but wait until tomorrow says a special meeting of our Debating Society; tomorrow we'll be in KERULA – lots of coconut trees, people have fairer skins and everything is so much smarter. Different again, then.

We stand on the platform, the two railwaymen and me. "15 minutes ahead of time – not bad after 500 miles," says the man

ONE WAY or ANOTHER

from HQ. "Does this happen in the UK?" I dare not answer.

Security may be a problem, but I cannot be sure. Certainly thieving is a temptation. But that's true of anywhere. Last thing at night a couple of soldiers walk up and down, presumably to deter any would-be robbers. We also have wire hooks under our bunks to fasten down our luggage (although nobody does). To be honest, it feels safer to me here than on the subway in London.

Tonight the debating society kids me into eating a boiled egg biriani for supper. It looks awful – but I gulp it down. My stomach goes into convulsions soon after, and only then do I notice they all had something else!

The train is slowing. Word from our railwaymen is that last night's rain has caused a mudslide which is blocking much of the track. It's true, too. When we get to the spot, there's a multitude of men, women and children beavering away to get the line clear. They will be paid next-to-nothing, but will be glad to be doing something, I am told. We have to take a detour.

There's not much further to go. I am headed for the end of the line – Kanniyakumari, the most southerly point of India. From there it isn't much of a distance to where my daughter is. I call her on the cellphone to say I won't be long … and feel a new embarrassment about this modern gadget, which so many of us take for granted, when I think of all the poverty I've seen.

Mostly the track is down to a single line now and the once-mighty express is running at a gentle pace. I busy myself hanging out of an open doorway taking pictures. Being the only westerner aboard has earned me a certain notoriety and people I've never met come up to me on platform stops and want to pose for photographs for this "crazy engleeesh journalist."

But now, at last, the journey is over for there are the buffers which say that this really is the end of the line.

A glance at my watch tells me its 4.25pm – 49 hours to the minute since this wonderful journey began and, despite the delays and diversions, a mere 60 minutes behind schedule. The man from the railway HQ would be very proud of that.

© Richard Meredith and Mercury Books – all rights reserved

Printed in the United Kingdom
by Lightning Source UK Ltd.
1756